CULTURE SMART!

PORTUGAL

THE ESSENTIAL GUIDE TO CUSTOMS & CULTURE

SANDY PINTO BASTO

KUPERARD

"The real voyage of discovery consists not in seeking new landscapes, but in having new eyes."

Adapted from Marcel Proust, *Remembrance of Things Past.*

ISBN 978 1 78702 333 8

British Library Cataloguing in Publication Data
A CIP catalogue entry for this book is available
from the British Library

First published in Great Britain
by Kuperard, an imprint of Bravo Ltd
59 Hutton Grove, London N12 8DS
Tel: +44 (0) 20 8446 2440
www.culturesmart.co.uk
Inquiries: publicity@kuperard.co.uk

Design Bobby Birchall
Printed in Turkey

SANDY PINTO BASTO was born in Lisbon but spent much of her early life abroad, living and studying in cities in Europe and Canada. She has a communications degree from McGill University in Montreal, Canada, and works as a bicultural translator, writer, and editor. Since 2014, Sandy has also specialized as a relocation consultant in Lisbon and Porto, helping foreigners settle in Portugal and adapt to their new cultural environment. Today Sandy divides her time with her family between Lisbon and Cascais.

CONTENTS

Legend has it that when Caesar's general arrived on Portuguese soil in the first century CE, he claimed to have discovered a lovely country blessed with a mild climate and a beautiful coastline, but whose inhabitants were ungoverned and ungovernable. The Portuguese are still impulsive and set in their ways, but they are ever charming, romantic, and nostalgic, with an unshakable loyalty toward family and friends. Their national pride is easily roused, and celebrations of their history and heritage burst forth at every opportunity. This is, after all, the nation of Vasco da Gama and Henry the Navigator—whose daring explorers were the first to round the Cape of Good Hope, discover the maritime route to the Orient, and colonize lands in South America, Africa, and Asia. *Culture Smart! Portugal* reveals a country that, having enjoyed periods of great power and influence, and endured times of economic hardship and political turmoil, has regained prosperity and international respect, and is eager to forge new paths.

Portugal is a land of contrasts and contradictions. Opulence dwells side by side with simplicity. Elegant homes nestle inside old, seemingly decrepit buildings. Lush green hills blend with jagged landscapes. The people themselves are colorful, diverse, and multifaceted. Take the time to get to know them, and you'll find them hardworking and eager to please. *Culture Smart! Portugal* takes you beneath the surface of this fascinating country and shows you how to blend in and make the most of your visit. In these pages, you'll gain insight into Portuguese priorities and values and learn how to tap into a helpful and resourceful nature that is often overlooked by the casual visitor.

At home and in business, the Portuguese are self-deprecating, fatalistic, and individualistic, in an unthreatening and even amusing way that can be both frustrating and enchanting. Beneath a seemingly gruff manner, they are laid-back and gentle. Tourists and foreigners are welcomed with enthusiasm, and hosts are eager to show off the best their country and culture has to offer, with a great sense of pride in the particular quality of life that is found here. So slacken your pace, put away your watch, and enjoy the rich meals, lively festivals, and ancient traditions. Make yourself available, and experience firsthand how guests in Portugal are treated as privileged members of the family.

Official Name	República Portuguesa (Republic of Portugal)	Member of the European Union and NATO
Capital City	Lisboa (Lisbon)	
Main Cities	Porto, Coimbra, Faro	
Area	35,580 sq. miles (92,152 sq. km)	
Geography	Situated on the westernmost tip of Europe, bordered to the north and east by Spain, and to the south and west by the Atlantic	
Climate	Mild (Mediterranean)	Summer spans July to mid-September.
Currency	The euro, since January 1999	Previously the Portuguese escudo
Population	10.1 million	
Ethnic Makeup	95% Portuguese	
National Language	Portuguese	Barranquenho is a dialect spoken only in the southern area of Barrancos, and Mirandês is a dialect used only on the northeastern border with Spain.
Religion	81% Roman Catholic	Other Christian 3.3%; Jewish, Muslim, plus other 0.6%; none 6.8%, unspecified 8.3%
Government	Democratic republic with the president as head of state and the prime minister as leader of government	Presidential elections are held every five years. Parliamentary elections are held every four years.

Economy	Service-based mixed economy with substantial privatization of state-controlled firms	An OECD member, Portugal is considered a High Income Economy.
Export	Main exports include vehicles and parts, electrical machinery, mineral fuels, plastics, and paper.	Top export destinations include Spain, France, Germany, USA, and the UK.
Import	Main imports include crude petroleum, vehicles, machinery, plastics, and steel.	Main source countries are Spain, Germany, France, Italy, and Netherlands.
Media	The national public television networks are RTP1 and RTP2, and the main private networks are SIC and TVI, as well as a number of private sports and news channels.	The main daily newspapers are *Diário de Notícias* (Lisbon), *Jornal de Notícias* (Porto), and *Público*. The main weekend papers are *Expresso* and *Semanário*.
Media: English Language	The *Portugal News* and *Portugal Resident*	
Electricity	220 volts, 50 Hz	Two-prong plugs are used. Transformers are required for US appliances.
Internet Domain	.pt	
Telephone	Portugal's country code is 351.	To dial out of Portugal, dial 00 followed by the country code.
Time	Greenwich Mean Time, five hours ahead of US Eastern Standard Time	

CHAPTER ONE

LAND & PEOPLE

GEOGRAPHY

Portuguese territory is divided between continental
Portugal, at the westernmost tip of the Iberian
Peninsula, and the archipelagos of the Azores
and Madeira in the Atlantic Ocean. Continental
Portugal shares borders with Spain to the north
and east, while the western and southern extremities
dive directly into the Atlantic.

On the continent, Portugal spans 349 miles
(561 km) at its longest and 135 miles (218 km)
at its widest, making it a small rectangle that can
be quite easily covered in a short amount of time.
The frontiers are partly defined by the four major
rivers, the Minho and the Douro in the north, and
the Tagus (Tejo) and the Guadiana in the south.
Elsewhere they are marked by mountain ranges.

Filled with churches, museums, shops, cafés, and traditional houses set along narrow cobbled streets, Lisbon's historic Alfama district is an explorer's paradise.

The continental territory is divided into eighteen districts, with each district's capital city bearing that district's name. The districts from north to south are Viana do Castelo, Braga, Vila Real, Bragança, Porto, Aveiro, Viseu, Guarda, Coimbra, Leiria, Castelo Branco, Santarém, Portalegre, Lisbon, Setúbal, Évora, Beja, and Faro.

Madeira is situated 566 miles (910 km) southwest of Lisbon and is comprised of the islands of Madeira and Porto Santo, which make up the Funchal district. The Azores archipelago lies 769 miles (1,238 km) west of Lisbon and is formed by the Horta, Angra do Heroísmo, and Ponta Delgada districts, with a total of nine islands.

Set on the banks of the Douro River, Porto's medieval Ribeira neighborhood is a UNESCO World Heritage Site and one of Europe's oldest city centers.

The capital, Lisbon, is situated on the coast in the middle of the national territory, at the mouth of the Tagus River. Lisbon's history spans over twenty centuries, and this is still visible today. Although Lisbon is a modern and cosmopolitan city, one can still relive the old classical traditions in the ancient neighborhoods of narrow cobblestone streets and medieval architecture where old houses still stand alongside ancient palaces and grand churches.

Following the coast north, to where the Douro River meets the Atlantic, is Porto. Portugal's second city, it has a dynamic business and cultural life.

The differences that distinguish Lisbon and Porto could at first glance hint at a certain rivalry between the two cities, but they actually complement each other. Whereas Lisbon at first comes across as a very classical, traditional city, the people are more modern, cosmopolitan, and open-minded. Porto, on the other hand, is outwardly modern in terms of aesthetics and sense of style (architecture, art, décor, fashion), yet at heart its inhabitants are very traditional and home-loving.

CLIMATE AND WEATHER

Despite its relatively small size, continental Portugal's climate varies significantly from region to region, with pronounced differences in temperature between the north and the south as well as between the coast and the territories further inland. Generally, however, the climate is mild, with daily temperatures ranging between 46.4°F and 64.4°F (8°C and 18°C) in the winter and 60.8°F and 86°F (16°C and 30°C) in the summer.

As with almost everything to do with Portugal, the climate can be divided into north, center, and south. The north registers higher precipitation with more rain and lower temperatures, whereas south of the Tagus River, due to the Mediterranean influence, the winters are shorter and drier and the summers hotter. The climate in the center, of course, lies somewhere in between. It is inland in the mountainous regions, however, where the climate ranges between bitter cold and snow in the winter and a parched, overbearing heat in the summer.

The Madeira Islands boast a typically Mediterranean climate, with mild temperatures and conditions all year round, whereas the Azores, while also mild, have a more bracing maritime climate and an abundance of rain.

REGIONS

Though culturally the Portuguese divide their country into north, center, and south, Portugal is divided into eight geographic regions, plus the Madeira and Azores archipelagos, which are, for administrative purposes, each considered "autonomous regions."

Entre Douro e Minho

The Minho and Douro Rivers give the northwestern region its name, Entre Douro e Minho. Translated literally as "Between Douro and Minho," this region includes the Viana do Castelo, Braga, Porto, and northern Aveiro districts. Usually referred to only as "Minho," the coastal area is flat, whereas further inland it becomes hilly and mountainous. The

Basilica of the Sacred Heart of Jesus overlooking the city of Viana do Castelo in the region of Entre Douro e Minho.

Minhoto culture is rich in tradition and folklore that is most evident during the local festivals.

Trás-os-Montes e Alto Douro

Directly East of Minho lies the Trás-os-Montes e Alto Douro region, also shortened to simply "Trás-os-Montes" for practicality. This region encompasses Vila Real, Bragança, northern Viseu, and northern Guarda. Its agriculture consists mainly of almond trees and the vines that produce grapes for the famous Port and Douro wines. This region is rich in traditional dialects that can make the locals quite difficult to understand.

A demarcated wine region since 1756, Douro Valley is home to dozens of terraced vineyards set among the picturesque hills of the Trás-os-Montes region.

Beira Interior

South of Trás-os-Montes is the Beira Interior region, which is formed by southern Guarda and the Castelo Branco district. The summer here can be very hot, but in the winter this is where the coldest temperatures register, often dropping below zero with snow in the mountain ranges.

These regions comprise what is generally referred to as "the north." The inhabitants of this area often have to move to the larger cities for work, but are extremely attached to their hometowns and roots. People from the north are typically hot-blooded, quick-tempered, and very straightforward. They keep their relationships simple, expressing their thoughts and emotions in a rowdy and often harsh manner, but once an issue has been dealt with, they move on. The reigning philosophy is to forgive and forget, and their loyalty and friendship has no bounds—though they expect the same in return.

Beira Litoral

Next to Beira Interior, toward the coast, southern Aveiro and Viseu, Coimbra, and parts of Leiria form the Beira Litoral. The land here is flat by the coast but becomes rocky inland. In this region industrial

The traditional shale village of Piodao nestled among the Serra do Açor mountain range, Coimbra.

activity abounds, but the area is renowned primarily for its architectural beauty. Coimbra University was the first in Portugal. Located in Lisbon at its inception in 1290 and then relocated to its present site in 1537, it is one of the oldest universities in Europe.

Estremadura e Ribatejo

Between the Beiras and Lisbon lies the Estremadura e Ribatejo region. This is an area where fertile soils, watered by the Tagus River, produce an abundance of fruit, vegetables, grain, tomatoes, olives, and vines. Horse and bull breeding is also concentrated here, and there are many enthusiastically attended agricultural fairs and bullfights. This small, wealthy region holds the country's highest concentration of World Heritage sites, such as Alcobaça, Batalha, Fátima, and Mafra.

Lisboa e Setúbal

The Lisboa e Setúbal region is made up of those two districts. It is here that the rivers Tagus and Sado are found. This is one of the better-known regions and is a tourist attraction due to its pleasant climate, green countryside, and beautiful beaches.

The area known as "the center" lies roughly between Setúbal and Coimbra. Here the people have a more modern and cosmopolitan attitude that can make them come across as aloof and inaccessible in comparison to their northerly neighbors. Friendships may seem more superficial, but this is primarily due to a more reserved and temperate nature. Feelings are either kept hidden or expressed in a more diplomatic manner, though there is always the possibility that someone is holding a grudge.

Alentejo

The Alentejo region is the largest district and includes southern Setúbal, Beja, Évora, and Portalegre. The land is mostly flat and dry, due to little rain and an extreme heat in the summer that imbues its

Shrouded in cloud and overlooking Europe's largest manmade lake is the walled town and fourteenth-century castle of Monsaraz, Alentejo.

inhabitants with a laid-back demeanor. Alentejanos are a typically rural population and generally keep to themselves. Life here revolves around the dining table and, as in the Ribatejo, local fairs are very popular. Although this region is primarily dedicated to farming, the coast is wild and beautiful, and tourism has also become a significant part of the economy, with visitors coming to enjoy the region's natural beauty and relaxed lifestyle. The Alentejo is a popular destination for those looking for an authentic Portuguese experience.

The Algarve region, characterized by a hilly Atlantic coastline, whitewashed fishing villages, and hidden sandy coves.

Algarve

At the southernmost tip of Portugal lies the Algarve, made up wholly of the Faro district. Other than Lisbon, this is probably the best-known region since it showcases the warm weather and picture-perfect beaches that Portugal is famous for. The lack of rivers and proximity to the Mediterranean make this area drier and hotter than the regions further north, offering sunny blue skies and beautiful beaches year-round.

The Alentejo and Algarve are what make up "the south," where a permanently procrastinating and laid-back attitude pervades. Away from the coast people often live on properties that may be miles from their closest neighbor or town, and this brings about a tendency to socialize little and keep to oneself. Foreigners and strangers are treated as just that and are usually kept at a comfortable distance. However, closer to the coast and the touristy areas, inhabitants are more aware that their livelihoods largely depend on visitors, a fact that was viscerally felt during the early stages of the coronavirus pandemic, when travel restrictions were in place. Aside from the vibrant tourism trade, this region has seen a major boom in foreign residents purchasing second homes or moving here for their retirement. As such, a concerted effort is made by all to communicate and engage, and it's common for most locals to speak at least a little English or German.

A BRIEF HISTORY

Early Inhabitants

The Iberian Peninsula's location between the Atlantic Ocean, the Cantabrian Sea (the southern part of the Bay of Biscay), and the Mediterranean provides an easy link between the European and African continents. This, as well as the mild and pleasant climate, has made it especially attractive for passage and settlement by many peoples down the ages.

The earliest inhabitants to leave their mark were the races of the Neolithic culture, believed to have traveled to the Iberian Peninsula from Asia Minor between 3,000 and 4,000 BCE in search of minerals. Remnants

A 5,000-year-old neolithic dolmen in Alentejo.

of dolmens (large stone chamber tombs) produced
by this culture can still be found in the Algarve
and Andalusian Spain. The Phoenicians, who were
traders and navigators, arrived around the twelfth
century BCE, followed by the Iberians. Though the
Iberians, to whom the peninsula owes its name, are
believed to have first migrated to the Ebro Valley
from North Africa in the Iron Age, their presence
in Portugal in historical records dates to around the
sixth century BCE, settling after the Phoenicians.

Around the seventh century BCE the Greeks,
also merchants, arrived, followed a century later by
the Celts from central Europe. The Celts held an
enormous advantage over the earlier inhabitants in
that they were skilled ironworkers. Whereas previous
settlers had come in search of copper and tin to
transform into bronze, iron could be used not only
for adornments and arms but also to make farming

tools; with crops growing and hunger diminishing, the population thrived. The Celts were also gifted goldsmiths and from them the Portuguese would inherit their craftsmanship and the traditional *Minhoto* (meaning "from Minho") filigree designs that are still created and worn today.

The Carthaginians, descendants of the Phoenicians, settled in the territory around the third century BCE, and dedicated themselves mainly to commerce and salting fish. The Romans expelled them that same century, during the Punic Wars. The fusion of these rich and diverse cultures—primarily between the Celts and the Iberians, who produced a race called the Celtiberians—created the people the Romans referred to as the Lusitanians. They were the tribe who occupied Lusitania, the lands that stretched between the Tagus and Douro Rivers. They were considered "the strongest of all the Iberian nations" and remained known throughout history for their courage and bravery. The word *Lusitano* is still used today to describe all things Portuguese.

The Romans

When the Romans invaded the Iberian Peninsula in 219 BCE, they found Celts north of the Douro River and Lusitanians between the Douro and Tagus Rivers. It was the Lusitanians, led by a humble but courageous shepherd named Viriato, who offered

Remains of a first-century CE Roman *villa rustica*, Belmonte.

them the greatest resistance and whose name would become a symbol of Portuguese independence.

The Roman presence lasted approximately seven centuries. During this time they founded cities—Olispo (Lisbon), Bracara (Braga), Scalabis (Santarém)—and built roads, bridges, and monuments, some of which still exist today. The founding of schools led to the spread of literacy and, from Latin, the local people under Roman influence created a dialect that would eventually become the Portuguese language.

Vandals and Visigoths

In the year 416 CE, while the Romans were fighting barbarian invasions on several fronts, the Suebi and the Vandals occupied the Iberian Peninsula. They in turn were pushed into the northwest and eventually conquered by the Visigoths. The Germanic kingdoms lasted for three centuries, adopting the existing Roman social, administrative, and economic structures. They also introduced laws concerning the ownership and inheritance of land, which led to a stratified society based on wealth and birth. Thus were cast the fundamental social divisions of clergy, nobility, and the people, a model that would later be adopted by medieval Portuguese society.

The Vandals and Visigoths subscribed to Arianism, a heretical form of Christianity, and persecuted the native Catholic Church. This complicated even further the fusion between the Germanic cultures and the Christian Hispano-Romans, until 589 CE, when King Reccared and all the Visigoths converted from Arianism to Catholicism. Thereafter the Christian kings of Spain, divinely appointed, worked closely with the Church to form an ideology of kingship.

The Moors

In the seventh century, the Arabs swept out of the Arabian Peninsula to spread the new religion of Islam by conquest. In 711 CE the Moors—Arabs and converted Berbers from North Africa—sailed across the narrow sea and overran the Iberian Peninsula. There they would remain for over five centuries. Apart from an undefeated Visigothic remnant in the inhospitable north, which formed the nucleus of resistance, Portugal and Spain were absorbed into the Umayyad Caliphate.

The eighth-century Castle of the Moors, perched upon a peak in the Sintra Hills, Lisboa region.

In the ninth century the Christian kingdoms of the northeast began a centuries-long counteroffensive known as the *reconquista*, and the Caliphate of Cordova, after a period of internal strife, eventually disintegrated into a number of independent kingdoms. The Christian advance was checked by the Moroccan Almoravids in the late eleventh and early twelfth centuries, and again in the 1150s by the sectarian Shi'ite Almohads.

By and large, Muslim rule was benign. The Moors produced a brilliant, multiethnic civilization in the Iberian Peninsula that stimulated the search for knowledge, allowed freedom of worship, and ushered in a period of cultural and intellectual cross-fertilization. Their treatment of their subject peoples depended on the attitude of those peoples toward the Islamic religion. If they converted, they were accepted into the community with equal rights and duties. If they maintained their Christian faith, they could own land and practice their religion, though with limitations, and were obliged to pay a tax. If they resisted with arms, they were either slaughtered or sold into slavery.

Moorish influence was greatest in the south and is still evident today in the whitewashed houses and rounded chimneys typical of the Algarve. The Moors also added new vocabulary to the existing Roman language, and brought about economic and technical renewal—for instance, by the use of the Alcatruz wheel to raise water from the riverbeds to channels for irrigation.

Kings and Kingdoms

The expansion of the Christian Kingdom of León in the twelfth century liberated much of Portugal. While the Almoravid caliphs were reestablishing Muslim control of the south, in the north Alfonso VI, King of León and Castile, enlisted foreign nobles to his cause. To his aid came the cousins Raymond and Henry of Burgundy (Raimundo and Henrique de Bourgogne), descendants of Robert II, King of France. As a token of his thanks, Alfonso gave Raimundo his daughter Urraca's hand in marriage as well as the county of Galicia, and to Henrique he gave his daughter

Teresa and the county of Portucale (Portugal), which stretched between the Minho and Tagus Rivers.

Henrique made Guimarães the capital of Portucale and ruled as a vassal of Alfonso, securing the Galician marches from Moorish raids. He held the firm desire to turn the county into an independent kingdom, but died in 1112 before seeing his dream realized. Upon his death, Teresa governed as regent, their son Afonso Henriques being only three years old. At the age of thirteen Afonso Henriques declared himself king and vowed to gain independence from León. In 1128 he seized control from his mother, who remained loyal to the Galician court, defeating her at the battle of São Mamede. For nine years he fought Alfonso VI of León, and in 1139, after a great victory over the Moors at Ourique, he was crowned Afonso I, first king of an independent Portugal. Finally, in 1143, through the Treaty of Zamora, Alfonso recognized Portugal as an independent kingdom.

Afonso Henriques became known as "the Conqueror" because his successful campaigns against the Moors expanded the kingdom to the south. After the battle of Ourique in 1139, he created a banner with five small blue shields representing the five Moorish kings he had defeated, and in each blue shield he placed five white dots representing the five wounds of Christ. This coat of arms remains at the center of the modern Portuguese flag. In 1147

Afonso captured Lisbon with the help of a Crusader fleet, and he later defeated the Moors twice at Santarém, in 1171 and 1184. He founded a chivalric order, the Order of Aviz, in about 1162.

Afonso's heirs continued to campaign against the Moors in the south until their final defeat in 1249 by Afonso III, when the Algarve was added to Portugal. Attempted incursions by the Marinid Sultanate of Morocco were decisively defeated by Afonso IV of Portugal and Alfonso XI of Castile in 1340.

Toward the end of the fourteenth century, Portugal was in crisis, having suffered greatly from the plague and finding itself at risk of losing independence to Castile once again. The conflict between the Christian monarchs of the Iberian Peninsula was further fueled by the Hundred Years' War between England and France. In the interregnum that followed the death in 1383 of Ferdinand I, last king of the House of Burgundy, John (Juan) of Castile claimed the Portuguese throne for himself and laid siege to Lisbon. The regent, Ferdinand's half-brother John (João), the Grand Master of Aviz, defeated the Spanish and was crowned king, as João I. Thus began the Aviz dynasty. Reinforced by English archers, João defeated the Castilians at the battle of Aljubarrota and ushered in a period of reform at home and discovery and expansion overseas. He made a treaty of friendship with England, and in 1387 married

Philippa of Lancaster, daughter of John of Gaunt, so initiating Portugal's earliest alliance with Great Britain.

A Love Story

Dom Pedro and Inês de Castro were Portugal's real-life Romeo and Juliet. Inês, a beautiful Spanish noblewoman, became lady-in-waiting to Constance of Castile when the latter traveled to Lisbon in 1340 to marry Dom Pedro, the crown prince and heir to the Portuguese throne. Dom Pedro and Inês fell in love, and though Pedro's father, King Afonso IV, banished her from the court, their love affair continued. When Constance died in 1345, Dom Pedro settled with Inês in Coimbra, where she bore him four children. Afonso maintained his opposition to the relationship and, in his son's absence, had Inês murdered. Distraught with grief and anger, Dom Pedro led a rebellion against his father, and on his death, when he was crowned King in 1357, had his lover's assassins murdered and tore their hearts out with his bare hands.

This tragic and romantic story is a favorite among the Portuguese, and has been featured widely in classical Portuguese literature.

THE ALJUBARROTA BAKER

Brites de Almeida, a local baker, became a
popular historical figure when, on August 14,
1385, she contributed to the Portuguese victory
in the Battle of Aljubarrota. Brites discovered
seven Castilians hidden in her oven. Legend
has it that she killed all seven with her baker's
paddle, and since then, the spade remains the
town's banner.

The Age of Discovery and Exploration

It was João and Philippa's sons, Duarte, Pedro,
and Henrique, who proposed discovering what lay
beyond Cape Bojador on the Atlantic coast of Africa,
and the capture and conversion of the Moroccan
city of Ceuta in 1415. Henrique, the famous
Henry the Navigator, then settled in Sagres in the
Algarve, where he founded a nautical school and
surrounded himself with cartographers, astronomers,
geographers, mathematicians, navigators, and
shipbuilding specialists. From here, expeditions
would set sail and Portugal would amass a vast
commercial and colonial empire spread throughout
Africa, Asia, and South America.

Thus, in 1419 the Portuguese discovered
Madeira, in 1427 the Azores, in 1456 Cabo Verde

and Guinea, and in 1471 São Tomé and Principe. João II, the "perfect prince," coordinated all known navigational knowledge, drawing on Arab and Jewish mathematical and astronomical sources, in what has been called the "first scientific revolution," so laying the foundations of European science a century later. Under João II's guidance the Portuguese continued to explore Africa's Atlantic coast, and in 1488 Bartholomeu Dias rounded the Cape of Torments at the southern point of Africa, which João renamed the "Cape of Good Hope." In July of 1497 Vasco da Gama set sail from Lisbon; less than a year later he anchored at India's great commercial

The departure of fifteenth-century explorer Vasco de Gama on his voyage to India, by Portuguese painter Roque Gameiro (1864–1935).

port of Calicut. The maritime route to India had finally been discovered. In 1500 Pedro Alvares Cabral reached Brazil, and between 1519 and 1521 Fernão de Magalhães (Ferdinand Magellan) became the first mariner ever to circumnavigate the globe.

Losing and Restoring Independence

In the mid-1500s Portugal entered a period of decline. The expulsion, or forcible conversion, of the Jews in 1497 deprived it of its middle class and of its most talented traders and financiers. Large numbers settled in Holland, where they contributed greatly to the success of the rival Dutch commercial empire. The Holy Office, or Inquisition, was established in Lisbon in 1536 to root out heresy.

In 1521, with the accession of John (João) III, the throne passed to the Habsburgs and came to be increasingly dominated by the Jesuits. The unworldly young king Sebastião launched a disastrously ill-prepared crusade against the Moors in Morocco that culminated in his death and the loss of the battle of Alcácer Quibir in 1578.

The vacuum created by this turn of events led to the invasion of Portugal by a Spanish army under the Duke of Alva, and in 1580 to the loss of independence to Philip II's Spain. Portugal was subject to the "Sixty Years' Captivity," during which time the country's finances, commerce, agriculture, and navy were ruined and the overseas empire abandoned. On December 1, 1640, a group of forty Portuguese noblemen, disgusted and frustrated with this neglect, stormed the viceroy's palace and the country united in the struggle to occupy forts and expel the Spanish troops. Two weeks later, João IV of the House of Braganza was proclaimed king.

The main goals following the restoration of independence were to keep foreign forces at bay, reorganize the country's economy, and attempt to regain some of the territories lost overseas. The Dutch were driven out of Brazil, and Portugal recovered its standing among European nations. Peace was finally settled between Spain and Portugal in 1668, and in 1703 the Methuen Treaty was signed with England, allowing Portugal to export wines to Britain and opening up the Portuguese market to English textiles. Also during this time, gold and diamonds were discovered in Brazil, filling the Portuguese coffers and funding many important works such as the building of Mafra's convent and Lisbon's aqueduct, as well as libraries, academies, and museums.

The Lisbon Earthquake
On November 1—All Saints' Day—1755, a huge earthquake shook Lisbon, almost totally destroying the city, killing an estimated 20,000 people, and terrorizing the population. The scale of the disaster

caused shockwaves throughout Europe, both actual and metaphorical, leading many people to doubt the wisdom of divine providence and also to question social certainties. Others saw it as divine wrath, a terrible warning to sinners. The timid King José Manuel's ruthless, yet clear-sighted and practical prime minister, Sebastião José de Carvalho, later made the Marquis of Pombal, took charge of the situation and rebuilt the capital as an elegantly planned modern city dedicated to commerce and industry. He set up a government of technocrats, reduced the power of the Inquisition, expelled the Jesuits, introduced secular education, reorganized the county's finances, and promoted trade.

The Long Decline

In 1807 Napoleon's armies invaded Portugal and the court fled to Brazil. Portuguese forces fought the French from 1807 to 1811, and with England's help forced them to withdraw. The Anglo-Portuguese troops were led by Sir Arthur Wellesley (later the Duke of Wellington), who was given three important Portuguese titles as a sign of gratitude for his aid.

In the years that followed, Portugal suffered great internal turmoil. In 1820 the liberal revolution forced the king to return from Brazil and accept constitutional government. Brazil declared independence in 1822. In 1826 the Constitution was replaced with a more conservative document. In 1828,

Queen Maria's accession was blocked by her uncle, Dom Miguel, who declared himself an absolute monarch. Civil war broke out between liberals and conservatives. In 1834 Queen Maria regained her throne with British, French, and Brazilian help, and constitutional government was restored. However, recurrent epidemics of cholera and yellow fever had begun, and would continue to decimate the population until the late 1850s. In the 1840s there were severe disputes between radicals and liberals. In 1851 the Duke of Saldanha staged a coup and launched a program of "regeneration" to promote order and economic growth. The late nineteenth century saw severe financial difficulties and the rise of socialist, anarchist, and republican parties.

In 1885 the Berlin Treaty, signed by the major imperial powers, stipulated that Africa should be shared among European nations, with Portugal taking control of the territories between Angola and Mozambique. In 1890, however, Great Britain gave Portugal an ultimatum, threatening to invade the Portuguese colonies if Portugal refused to remove its troops from the Chire valley, in Chiromo, near Mozambique. Being at a military disadvantage, Portugal was forced to acquiesce. King Carlos I suspended the Constitution in 1907 and installed João Franco as dictator. Discontentment with Franco's measures led to the first attempt to install a republican regime. Carlos and his heir Luis Filipe were assassinated in the streets of Lisbon in 1908. Carlos's second son took the throne as Manuel II, but for only a short time. Two years later a republican revolution forced the royal family to flee to England.

The First Republic and the "Estado Novo"

On October 5, 1910, after a three-day insurrection, Portugal was proclaimed a republic. Although the new regime adopted a liberal Constitution in 1911, it involved several parties more interested in power than in progress, and the years that followed mark a period of economic hardship, corruption, and acute political instability. In 1916, Britain pressured Portugal into seizing around seventy German merchant ships seeking refuge in the Tagus, thus forcing Portuguese participation in the First World War on the Allied side in Africa to defend its colonies against Germany. The devastating impact of the war—inflation, food shortages, and the human toll in France—led to a coup in 1917 by Bernardino Sidónio Pais, who became the first republican dictator of the twentieth century. He was assassinated a year later, and the country was plunged into chaos. Finally, in 1926, seeing no end to the desperate situation, General Gomes da Costa led a military coup that established a dictatorship that was to last forty-eight years. In 1928, António de Oliviera Salazar became minister of finance. His reforms created economic stability, rebuilding the country's confidence, and renewing the world's respect for Portugal.

In 1933 Salazar was nominated president of the Ministers' Council, and the following year military rule ended. The authoritarian corporatist Estado Novo ("New State") he created initiated a period of national reconstruction, raising the value of Portuguese currency abroad, rebuilding the navy, building roads, ports, schools, and hospitals, and reviving agriculture and industry. However, fearful of atheist communism, Salazar resisted demands for democratic change at home and in the colonies and maintained order by means of an unrestrained secret police.

Thanks to Salazar, Portugal was spared involvement in the Second World War and went on to profit greatly from the export of raw materials, particularly tungsten, to both sides. In 1949 Portugal became a founding member of NATO. In 1961, however, the remaining Portuguese colonies in India—the cities of Goa, Damão, and Diu—were occupied by Indian forces. That same year, insurgency in Angola, Mozambique, and Guinea-Bissau brought on a debilitating colonial war that would last over a decade.

Spy Stories

With Portugal being neutral during the Second World War, Lisbon was filled with spies. If you head west from the capital and follow the coast toward Cabo da Roca, the westernmost tip of Europe, you will pass Estoril, a lovely seaside town on a coastline that has often been compared with the French Riviera. Estoril's casino, the largest in Europe at the time, was a favored spot for spies to meet and exchange intelligence. It was so common in fact that numerous authors, such as John le Carré and Graham Greene, as well as the film *The Russia House,* used Estoril as a setting for their spy stories.

The Peaceful Revolution

Incapacitated by a stroke, Salazar was relieved of his office in 1968 and was succeeded by Marcello Caetano. A former member of Salazar's cabinets, Caetano was a great admirer of his predecessor. Though he was successful in his social and economic reforms, Caetano's political strategies were heavily opposed. His more liberal colleagues, his opponents, and country people felt that he had failed to democratize Portugal sufficiently. Discontent was brewing beneath the surface, and on April 25, 1974, a group of captains and generals staged an uprising against the autocratic regime. What began as a coup quickly became a revolution. Political parties mushroomed. Exiles returned, political prisoners were released, and soldiers carried red carnations in the barrels of their guns. In May the junta handed over power to a fifteen-man provisional government. The colonial war was immediately ended

Civilians on a tank during the "Carnation Revolution," Lisbon, 1974.

and Portugal conceded independence to all the remaining colonies (except Macau), which, like Brazil, chose to retain Portuguese as their official language.

Portugal has since made giant strides in overcoming the malaise—the legacy of the decline of empire and the political unrest of the nineteenth century—that previously kept it apart from other developed nations. Entry into the European Economic Community (now the European Union) in 1986 had a profound impact on its economic development. Since then, Portugal has joined the global economy and gained greater international exposure, resulting in growing supply and demand, investment, exports, and public spending. One of the eleven founding members of the single European currency, Portugal's adoption of the euro in 1999 further enhanced this growth by lowering the national debt, inflation, and interest rates.

GOVERNMENT

Today Portugal is a pluralistic democracy in which the legislature, executive, and judiciary are fully separate. The president is head of state, and also commander in chief of the armed forces. He represents the Portuguese Republic and guarantees national independence, state unity, and the proper conduct of the democratic institutions. The president is elected for a five-year term of office and can serve a maximum of two consecutive terms. Parliament is a single-chamber assembly representative of all citizens. Portuguese citizens over the age of eighteen can participate in elections, whether they live in Portugal or abroad. In addition to its legislative function, parliament supervises enforcement of the

The seat of Portuguese parliament, the Palace of Saint Benedict, Lisbon.

Constitution and its laws and monitors the government and public administration. It consists of 230 deputies, elected by geographically defined constituencies for a four-year mandate. The government is made up of the prime minister, the ministers' council, and secretaries and subsecretaries of state. The president, based on the results of the parliamentary elections, nominates the prime minister, generally the leader of the party with the most votes.

THE ECONOMY

Despite a debilitating recession that lasted for over a decade, following the political unrest in the 1970s, Portugal experienced one of the highest rates of economic growth in Europe in the latter part of the twentieth century. The period of prosperity, however, came to an end when the global financial crisis of 2008 wreaked havoc on the country's finances, resulting in the adoption of a European bailout program that involved strict measures of austerity. The intervention was ultimately successful and in 2015 Portugal began its economic comeback. Until the outbreak of the coronavirus pandemic in 2020, Portugal had experienced record growth and investment in numerous sectors. By the end of 2021, the economy was back on a positive trajectory.

Traditionally an agriculture-based economy, today

only around 5 percent of the country's workforce is employed in the field and the sector accounts for only 2 percent of the country's GDP. Around 40 percent of land is still used for agriculture, however, with grain, potatoes, grapes (for wine), olives, and tomatoes being the main produce grown. Portugal is also a leading exporter of tomato paste and wine.

While other European nations underwent heavy industrialization throughout the nineteenth century, Portugal lagged behind. Industrialization occurred slowly and in spurts, encountering heavy opposition by landowners and the aristocracy and taking second place to colonial affairs. Thus, in the early twentieth century, over 80 percent of the population was still rural. Industrial expansion occurred more significantly under Salazar in the 1950s, and since then the economy has become progressively mixed. In more recent decades there has been a major shift toward manufacturing and in 2022 industry accounted for approximately 19 percent of the country's economic output. It wasn't all plain sailing: sectors like textiles and footwear were dominated by competitors in Asia, which forced Portugal to adapt to newer sectors that required greater technological incorporation, such as the automotive, electronics, and energy sectors, as well as new information and communication technology sectors. Increased foreign direct investment as a result of accession to the EU enabled Portugal to develop a strong services sector, primarily in finance and telecommunications, which has come to account for the vast majority of the country's GDP. Ongoing government investment in education and infrastructure has paid dividends, with many multinational corporations choosing to set up operations in the country in recent years. Less than a three-hour flight from most European capitals and with access to qualified, multilingual professionals at comparatively low cost, Portugal is an attractive choice for companies looking for an optimal location for their business services.

The resulting increase in foreign businesses, entrepreneurs, and professionals moving to Portugal has driven a major real estate boom, bringing an unprecedented wave of urban renewal and investment into the country's housing stock. Supply has struggled to match the surge in demand, though, and as a result property prices have risen to levels that can sometimes surprise foreigners. In addition, lower-earning Portuguese are increasingly finding themselves priced out of city centers.

COVID-19

Portugal's first documented cases of Covid-19 occurred in March 2020. Wary of the new disease, many took it upon themselves to reduce face-to-face activities until March 18, when the government declared a state of emergency and imposed a general lockdown for six weeks. A second lockdown was announced on January 15, this time for almost eight weeks. In addition, travel bans were imposed, as was a curfew limiting movement outside the home between 11 p.m. and 5 a.m.

Typically fearful of illness and disease, the Portuguese were highly respectful of the measures and city streets were eerily empty during the lockdowns. Vaccination rates were high and by the beginning of 2022, nearly the whole population had received at least two jabs. There was also a distinct lack of anti-vaxxers, in contrast to other southern European countries.

While there may not have been much rule breaking, there was plenty of characteristic rule bending: dogs were walked far beyond what was probably necessary (or permitted) and people who may never have exercised in their lives suddenly required numerous outings a day.

While most were resigned to comply with the measures for the greater good, government-sanctioned celebrations on the anniversary of the 1974 revolution in April 2020 caused some to accuse the authorities of hypocrisy. Overall, though, the combination of swift measures by the authorities and people's compliance allowed Portugal to weather the pandemic better than many other European countries and to emerge as something of an international public health success story.

CHAPTER TWO

VALUES & ATTITUDES

Portuguese society is close-knit and relationship-based, with the family at its core. Whether at work or play, personal contact is key. The Portuguese work to live, rather than vice versa, and any excuse to socialize and have fun is welcome. Yet while their capacity for pleasure is boundless, they also revel in nostalgia and cultivate fatalism. Open and friendly once at ease, they can be suspicious and defensive if feeling insecure or on unfamiliar terrain. Once you become accustomed to these contradictions, you will find them to be warm, outgoing people who are always ready for fun and celebration.

FAMILY

In the not-so-distant past it was common for traditional Portuguese families to be quite large, often having five or six children. As in the rest of Europe, however, over the last few decades Portugal has experienced a decline in its marriage and birth rates. In 2022 the average birth rate was 1.28 births per woman, which was below the European average of 1.61. Today, more are choosing to pursue higher education at university level, with many continuing to complete a Master's degree (in Portugal 33 percent of those at university are studying at Master's level, double the OECD average). It is only after completing their studies that a career is seriously embarked upon, and for many today, this takes precedence over starting a family. This is particularly the case for younger women. In 2022 the average age for a woman to have her first child in Portugal was thirty-two, compared to twenty-nine in 2012 and twenty-five in 1960.

Attitudes towards the institution of marriage are also changing among younger Portuguese, and an increasing number of women are choosing to delay or even forego marriage and childbearing in favor of their career and other personal pursuits, while others are content to cohabit for longer periods than in the past, without tying the knot. Indeed, rates of marriage in Portugal are now at an all-time low and among the lowest in Europe.

Despite all this, the concept of family remains a

central pillar of Portuguese society. Nuclear families are small (2.5 people on average), but the extended family is anything but. When a person refers to their family in Portugal, they're referring to a colorful array of grandparents, godparents, aunts, uncles, and cousins. This panoply of relatives may not necessarily reside under the same roof, but will generally live as close together as they can and maintain daily contact.

The importance of family is not born of affection alone, but of necessity, too. Until the early 1960s, women made up 20 percent of the working population, the accepted norm being that they should marry young and stay at home bearing and rearing children. Since then, female university attendance has risen to over 50 percent, and women today represent almost half the national workforce, occupy 40 percent of positions in government, and run close to 40 percent of all companies in Portugal. It is by and large thanks to the willingness of grandparents to step in as day care that this has been possible. Whether public or private, day care in Portugal is simply not an option for many families, and so grandparents are relied on to lend a hand—it's partly for this reason that in Portugal the elderly are both visible and respected, because they take such an active role in family life.

Portuguese families were traditionally seen as predominantly matriarchal, with the wife seen as making most of the domestic decisions. Today, however, the division of chores and duties has become more equal among younger couples and the traditional roles of "homemaker" and "provider" are no longer as clearly divided between mother and father. Today, both roles are often shared.

One aspect that has not changed, however, is that it's still as common for children to live at home until they marry. What does that mean in practice? Well, in 2022, 64 percent of people aged eighteen to thirty-four still lived at home, and though many of those will be in some form of employment, they are not expected to contribute to the household expenses, but rather to save for when they do eventually fly the nest, most often when they are in their late twenties and early thirties.

Children are considered the center of the household. Not infrequently, long work hours inspire a parental need to compensate their kids in some form or another. Parents often go without in order to provide their children with luxuries, with the effect that children can often end up somewhat spoiled and overprotected. It's uncommon to see these children in public without adult supervision since they are almost always accompanied to and from school or when playing outside, even when older. Being accustomed to adult company, children are usually sociable and confident and are often proudly paraded by their caretakers whenever possible.

Portuguese families value loyalty and discretion above all, and it is unacceptable to "air one's dirty laundry." Such large extended families, when reunited, can reach twenty or thirty individuals, and so it's natural that the occasional disagreement can arise. The Portuguese keep their personal issues to themselves and prefer to resolve them privately "*em família*" rather than make them public. If they do "*desabafar*" (get it off their chest), however, this is done in strict confidence, and it carries the implicit understanding that only family members are allowed to speak ill of the family.

RELIGION

Portugal is still a religious country. "*Se Deus quiser,*" translated as "God willing," is one of the most common endings to a Portuguese sentence. Almost 80 percent of the population is Roman Catholic, with 19 percent attending mass regularly. Although this is proof that religion is very much a part of people's lives, compared with the statistics fifteen years ago when 95 percent of the population was Roman Catholic and 50 percent attended mass at least once a month, there has been a clear decline in religious affiliation. Nonetheless, even those who only go to church for social events such as weddings, baptisms, funerals, and religious holidays will prepare themselves scrupulously and attend with enthusiasm. This, of course, is in the spirit of family unity, and any excuse for a reunion is welcome!

The Sanctuary of Christ the King monument, Lisbon. Built in 1959, it was inspired by the Christ the Redeemer statue in Rio de Janeiro, Brazil.

Though Catholicism is the dominant religion, the recent rise in immigration has brought about a cultural, ethnic, and religious diversity in which the Catholic Church now coexists peacefully with other religions.

The Miracle of the Roses

Isabel of Aragon (1269–1336), wife of King Dinis, was dubbed the Holy Queen and canonized in 1625 for the many miracles she performed. She was renowned for founding charities and hospitals, as well as visiting the poor and handing out coins and bread. The legend for which she is best remembered, the miracle of the roses, took place when she was concealing in her cloak a considerable amount of coins to give to the poor. This was an expensive practice of which the King did not approve. One day he intercepted her and asked her what she was carrying. When she opened her cape to show him, the coins had been transformed into roses, and so she simply replied, "Roses, my lord."

Fátima

The shrine of Fátima, near Leiria, is the religious heart of Portugal, drawing pilgrims from around the world throughout the year, who come to pray, give thanks, and strengthen their spiritual bond.

The story of the miracle of Fátima describes how, over a six-month period in 1917, the Virgin Mary appeared to three young shepherds in Fátima and made three prophecies. The first was the confirmation of the existence of Hell; the second was the end of the First World War, with Russia's abandoning of the Christian faith and embracing of communism, leading to war and persecution; and the third predicted an assassination attempt on Pope John Paul II.

After thirteen years of examination by clergy and scientists, in 1930 the Catholic Church pronounced the apparitions worthy of belief and the cult of Our Lady of Fátima was officially sanctioned. Fátima's shrine and its symbolism are now so strong that even though many people today are no longer aware of the original story of the miracles, its spiritual significance is great enough to attract multitudes of worshipers year after year.

FORMALITY AND RESPECT

Manners and etiquette in Portugal are considered a sign of respect and are therefore highly regarded. Today, the Portuguese are more lenient in this department as long as it's clear that no disrespect is intended. Foreigners are given the benefit of the doubt for being unfamiliar with local conduct, but if certain standards are practiced, your hosts will feel more comfortable and likely to accept you.

For example, when it comes to greeting, women kiss men and each other on one or both cheeks. Men shake hands and the closer they are or the happier they are to see each other, the more vigorous the handshake, often accompanied by a bear hug and loud slaps on the back. In parting, the same ritual is repeated though the hugs and back pats are usually softer by this point.

Certain courtesies are becoming rarer among younger Portuguese, having fallen out of style. For example, it's not uncommon to see an elderly man tip his hat in a lady's presence, or a gentleman greet an older lady by kissing her hand. Other points of etiquette hold fast and from an early age children are taught to treat adults respectfully. For example, hats are not worn indoors, youngsters are expected to stand up and greet elders when they enter a room, doing so again on parting, and so on. Though in theory adults and the elderly expect young people to behave appropriately, children's company is welcome and the attitude toward them is generally playful and permissive.

One example of the Portuguese affinity for formality and tradition is when a young couple decides to marry. Marriage in Portugal is not only the joining of two people, but is also expected to be the beginning of a lasting union between the bride and groom's families.

As a sign of respect, the groom may ask the bride's father for his daughter's hand in marriage. If choosing to abide by the more old-fashioned customs, he may meet with his future father-in-law in private and state his intentions. Or the young couple merely announce their decision and ask for their parents' blessing.

Once practical details regarding the wedding are decided upon and preparations are under way, a formal engagement celebration takes place, usually a few months before the marriage. This occasion is called the *pedido*, or proposal, and generally involves the bride's family inviting the groom's family for a meal. Here, the bride's father may make a speech welcoming the groom and his family into his household, followed by the groom who is also expected to address his future in-laws as well as formally propose to his bride and offer her an engagement ring. The *pedido* not only serves to make the engagement official, but also gives the families a chance to break the ice and get acquainted before the wedding day.

SOCIABILITY, SUSPICION, AND ACCEPTANCE

The Portuguese are at heart a sociable and friendly culture. As we've seen, the most important relationships are with one's family, but this is closely followed by friendships, which in Portugal are strong and often lifelong. The Portuguese love to socialize, which means that acquaintances are numerous and are also treated warmly. Different to friendships, however, these relationships are kept at a more superficial level, and most often, one's different social circles are kept separate.

Being as sociable as they are, most Portuguese like to place people within a specific social context in order to be able to make sense of and accept them. This means that they can be suspicious of strangers and, on first meeting someone, may seem cold and even unfriendly. It needn't take too long to break the ice, however. In many cases, going to the same grocer or having a mutual acquaintance or children the same age is enough to overcome the initial reserve. Foreign visitors are sometimes placed in a different framework that keeps them at bay. However, the quicker you adopt a "when in Rome" attitude and establish common ground, the sooner you'll benefit from the fun and warmth of being accepted as an equal.

Since the Portuguese are very proud of their food, eating their dishes with enthusiasm is guaranteed to elicit a positive response. If you see someone eating whole small fish with their fingers or avidly sucking shrimp heads, there's no need to make a face, it's just how things are done around here. Instead, try one yourself—you may be surprised! The Portuguese are very affectionate toward children, so a playful or tender gesture toward someone's child is sure to break down the parent's guard. Also, if you can be helpful in any way, this will warm people to you. For example, you could offer to carry an elderly neighbor's shopping bags home for them.

Overall, the Portuguese are curious and eager to please, and when interest is shown toward someone, it's genuine. Be open and communicative and they will make it their personal mission to ensure you enjoy yourself. For more on socializing, see Chapter 4.

MACHISMO AND EGALITARIANISM

Portuguese society seems at first glance male-dominated, but the underlying structure is definitely matriarchal. The men are hot-blooded Latinos at heart who love to size up and discuss the attributes of women in general. "Their" women, however, (that is, their mothers, sisters, wives, daughters, and girlfriends) are completely off-limits. Men will also behave differently when they are among themselves than when they are with female company. Male *machismo* is gradually changing, however, as society becomes more invested in gender equality.

In order to understand how *machismo* operates in society, it's worthwhile examining both the positive and negative aspects. On the one hand, most men see it as important to treat women "like ladies," such as by politely opening doors, pulling out chairs for them, refraining from crude language, and generally behaving well when around them and by themselves. On the other hand, when in the company of other men, they can be loud and obnoxious. This behavior, though provocative, is generally harmless and best ignored. Younger Portuguese men certainly behave in a more egalitarian way and in general are pushing for greater equality between the sexes. While there is still some way to go before true equality is achieved, the progress that has been made so far is palpable and today, more and more women feel empowered to live their lives on their own terms and are willing to put up with much less *machismo* behaviour than they may have in the past. One area where progress has been slower, however, is behind the wheel (see Chapter 6).

TOLERANCE AND PREJUDICE

The Portuguese consider themselves tolerant, but are not concerned with being politically correct. They are direct and speak their minds, sometimes regardless of whether what they say can be considered offensive, and are annoyed by people who beat around the bush or sugarcoat their opinions. Until fairly recently, most people's exposure to foreign cultures was somewhat limited, so if a derogatory remark is made, it's usually due to ignorance rather than a mean or hurtful intent.

As colonizers went, the Portuguese were considered to be at the fairer end of the spectrum and more inclusive when it came to social structure. Portugal also began emancipating slaves in 1761, well before other nations began to do the same. In the past, most Portuguese people's interaction with foreigners were with those from ex-colonies who had often suffered personal and economic hardships and who had moved to Portugal in search of work and a better life. They were also usually uneducated. It was these experiences that formed the basis for stereotypes that developed in Portugal. With the advent of mass tourism, global trade, and the media, however, old-time prejudicial attitudes are less commonly found, though they do still appear, from time to time.

Sexual tolerance has also become more widespread as time goes on, largely for the same reasons. In 2010, Portugal became the eighth country in the world to approve gay marriage and, in 2016, a bill legalising adoption by same-sex couples was also passed. In 2019, Portugal was voted as the world's most LGBTQ-friendly travel destination, along with Canada and Sweden.

People's tolerance does have its limits, though. For example, while there are nude beaches to be found along Portugal's coastline, public nudity on undesignated beaches is not appreciated. Many female tourists choose to go topless, and though this isn't necessarily reprimanded, most locals refrain from doing so themselves. Unless attending a nude beach or lucky enough to be on a deserted stretch, use a bathing suit of some kind and avoid changing into or out of your bathing suit in public.

INDIVIDUALISM AND NATIONAL PRIDE

Due to periods of political confusion and disruption throughout their history, and possibly as a form of self-preservation, the Portuguese have cultivated a certain individualism and fatalism. While providing a form of armory against the ups and downs of historical destiny, it has also led to a cynical and sometimes self-deprecating attitude. As you will soon pick up, the Portuguese love to speak harshly of their own country, and yet will sometimes act only to better their own situation rather than attempt to improve the common good. Thankfully, this isn't always the case, and a sense of community, when realized, has proven to be both effective and enduring.

One such example was the public response to the coronavirus pandemic. For over two years, the vast majority of people were willing to adapt to sometimes difficult changes in order to protect the vulnerable and the public health system, and to ensure the orderly continuation of daily life—well, as orderly as it could be under the circumstances. As at other points in Portugal's sometimes troubled history, a sense of community and national pride led the Portuguese to unite and work together to overcome an otherwise difficult period.

When all else fails, and people's individual attitudes seem to get the better of them, there is one thing that will always continue to unite the Portuguese, and that's soccer. When Portugal defeated France in the final of the Euro 2016 Championship, despite the absence of their captain Cristiano Ronaldo who was injured and carried off the pitch in the first twenty-five minutes of the match, the morale of the country sky-rocketed. The victory party, set off with blasts of red and green water cannons to welcome home the heroes, lasted for weeks.

All in all, the Portuguese have a strong sense of individual responsibility and self-reliance, but they also understand the importance of being part of a community. As a result, they are often described as being both independent and interdependent. This combination of individualism and community spirit is one of the contradictions that makes Portugal an interesting place to be. Oh, and one small caveat about

Portuguese self-deprecation: just as in family matters, while it may be acceptable for the Portuguese to criticize their own country, it certainly won't go down well for an outsider to do the same. Criticism and even observations that may seem critical are best saved until a solid relationship has been established.

SAUDADE

The Portuguese are a nostalgic people. They are as nostalgic for what used to be as they are for what could have been, and this bittersweet, romantic fatalism is what is implied by the term "*saudade*." Portuguese elders love to sigh and lament and dwell on woeful stories, yet at the same time they have a great capacity for joy. This is yet another example of the colorful and contradictory nature of a people who love to mourn their plight, yet have a perpetual sense of fun and enjoy boisterous celebrations at national, religious, and family occasions. The country's passion for nostalgia was reflected in its 2021 Eurovision Song Contest entry by singer and musician MARO. For those unacquainted with the Portuguese sense of *saudade*, the song is well worth a listen!

CHAPTER THREE

CUSTOMS & TRADITIONS

"*TÍPICO*"

The word "*típico*" is widely used and highly regarded in the Portuguese language. Translated literally as "typical," *típico* means anything traditionally, truly, typically Portuguese. There is typical everything: dishes, restaurants, customs, costumes, songs, dances … and these can vary from region to region or even town to town. These traditions have been cherished and maintained throughout the country's history and are proudly displayed during holidays and local festivals as an integral part of Portuguese culture.

PUBLIC HOLIDAYS

Portugal has fourteen public holidays throughout the year plus over a hundred municipal holidays.

The national holidays celebrate either a religious or historical event, while the municipal celebrations usually honor the town's patron saint, with one day taken off work and local festivities that can last a week or more. When a holiday's date falls on a Thursday or Tuesday, it is common to take the Friday or Monday off ("*fazer ponte*"—"make a bridge") and extend the holiday to form a long weekend.

RELIGIOUS HOLIDAYS

Christmas and Easter are the most important religious holidays. Extended families use the occasion to get together, going to mass and sharing lavish meals of traditional food and plenty of wine.

Midnight mass (*missa do galo*) is attended on Christmas Eve (unofficially also a holiday, except for retail businesses), usually followed by a *ceia* or evening meal. On December 25 the festivities continue with lunch and often dinner as well. The menus vary from region to region, but Christmas meals are typically comprised of cod-based dishes as well as the traditional roast turkey, with rich desserts and pastries heavy in butter and sugary egg yolks. It is normal for families to travel around a lot during these two days in an attempt to see as many relatives as possible, and gifts are exchanged

Commerce Square (Praça do Comércio), Lisbon, at Christmas time.

at each meeting. At this time of year, town and city centers are filled with lights, nativity scenes, and other traditional Christmas decorations. Most homes have a Christmas tree and nativity scene (*Presépio*) with Joseph, Mary, and Jesus in the manger, as well as figurines of shepherds, animals, and the three wise men. The more modern figure of Santa Claus has permeated the once strictly religious holiday and is also included in the public and private decorations and festivities.

Palm Sunday, one week before Easter Sunday, marks the beginning of Holy Week (*Semana Santa*).

Traditional Easter cake, Folar de Páscoa.

Customs vary from town to town and region to region, the older neighborhoods and rural areas being more "typical" and maintaining the more traditional ceremonies, but the principal rituals are upheld throughout the country. On Palm Sunday, the last day of Lent, each parish holds a procession celebrating Christ's entry into Jerusalem. Often the priest takes the opportunity to visit parish homes and families, and it is customary for children to give their godparents flowers. Throughout the week, a variety of processions are carried out parading statues of Jesus and Mary, and people hang their most elaborate and treasured embroidered blankets and cloaks outside their windows and balconies.

Good Friday, the anniversary of Christ's crucifixion, is a day of fasting and spiritual reflection. There are also local processions and plays that reenact the Passion of Christ. On Easter Sunday, churches are full and a general sense of celebration pervades. As is the case at Christmas, families unite for large, elaborate meals, and the international customs of offering and hunting for chocolate Easter eggs and rabbits are also practiced.

January 1	New Year's Day
February (always a Tuesday)	Carnival
March/April	Good Friday
March/April	Easter Sunday
April 25	Liberation Day
May 1	Labor Day
May/June	Corpus Christi
June 10	Portuguese National Day
August 15	Assumption Day
October 5	Proclamation of the Republic
November 1	All Saints Day
December 1	Restoration of Independence
December 8	Immaculate Conception
December 25	Christmas

Carnival in Podence, in the northeastern Trás-os-Montes region.

CARNIVAL

Carnival, or Entrudo, falls on the Tuesday before
Ash Wednesday and marks the last day before Lent.
Though not an official holiday, schools close on
Carnival Monday and Tuesday, and many companies
give their employees the day off. The Portuguese
celebration of Carnival varies greatly throughout
the country. Some cities, such as Loulé, choose to
copy the Brazilian concept of carnival, with street
dances and samba school competitions, while others
prefer putting local craftsmanship on display. In
some areas, celebrations are of a more ceremonial

and conservative nature, whereas in cities like Ovar or Torres Vedras, participants run loose, tickling and teasing onlookers or parading giant puppets that satirize historical figures and modern-day politicians. Generally, people use Entrudo as an excuse to dress up and have fun, be it publicly or privately, while others simply take the opportunity to get away and enjoy a long weekend.

POPULAR SAINTS

The month of June brings what is known as the Santos Populares, festivities of pagan origin celebrating the Summer Solstice. The favorite saints are Santo António (Saint Anthony), São João (Saint John), and São Pedro (Saint Peter), and though the reason these holy figures are associated with the summer folly is unknown, they have come to symbolize the connection between the sacred and the pagan. Between June and August, private and public balconies and patios all over the country are decked with lights, streamers, wild leeks, and potted basil. Communities come together to consume large quantities of grilled sardines, *caldo verde* (a traditional green cabbage soup), and wine in order to celebrate summer and ask the saints for good luck. The day following the celebrations is a municipal holiday.

Lisboetas celebrate the Feast of Santo António at numerous neighborhood *arraiais* around the city.

Santo António

Santo António was an exemplary Franciscan monk who was considered among other things to be the protector of the poor and of single girls, and a curer of infertility, the last two attributes endowing him with matchmaking qualities. Though not officially Lisbon's patron saint, he has been "adopted" by the city, and the festivities that honor him begin on June 12 with the Santo António weddings. Since 1950, the city of Lisbon has selected a group from among the city's poorer engaged couples to participate in a public wedding. After the ceremony, the couples are paraded around the city, stopping at the saint's statue to offer him the bride's bouquet before continuing on to the reception, also provided by the city.

Also taking place that night are Lisbon's *"Marchas Populares."* Avenida da Liberdade, one of downtown Lisbon's main avenues, sets the stage for a parade where over twenty associations representing the traditional neighborhoods compete in songs, choreography, and costumes. Each procession is an explosion of color and music that attempts to capture the essence of local tradition.

São João

In the north, the preferred saint is São João. As in the rest of the country, outdoor fairs and parties are organized where plenty of traditional singing and dancing takes place, with the night of São João being celebrated on June 23. In Porto, revelers roam the

Participants celebrate at the Rusgas de São João.

streets and squares armed with plastic hammers and wild leeks, banging them on the heads of passersby for good luck. It's best to maintain a sense of humor and take this in the spirit of excess and good fun! Aside from the neighborhoods competing with their displays of fireworks, it is also customary on this night for everyone to set large, colorful paper balloons alight and release them into the sky, watching them float, glowing, over the city.

FAMILY CELEBRATIONS

In the urban centers today family occasions are celebrated or marked in much the same way as in other cultures with Christian practices. Weddings, baptisms, and funerals in Portugal's small, rural communities, however, follow time-honored traditions.

Weddings

At Portuguese weddings—particularly those in rural regions—the bridal party (the bride's extended family and close circle of friends) will go to the bride's home for breakfast and then accompany her to the church for the wedding ceremony, while the same occurs at the groom's family home. After the ceremony, the guests are invited to a reception where a lunch consisting of numerous courses and large quantities of wine and other beverages is served. Following lunch and dancing, it is customary for everyone to visit the newlyweds' home and then go home themselves for a siesta before meeting up again for another meal, usually but not necessarily lighter than the lunch. Sometimes guests are invited back the following day for leftovers! Wedding guests are expected to give the newlyweds a gift. In some cases the bride and groom may have gift registries in shops where people can purchase items they have chosen beforehand, while in others, an envelope is passed around during the reception for guests to give money. In cities, where celebrations are less traditional, weddings are much like anywhere else in the West whereby there will be a ceremony held according to the couples' religion and beliefs, followed by a reception where the number of participants and degree of sophistication will depend on the budget. In all cases, there will be plenty of drinking, eating, and dancing into the early hours!

Baptisms

Because baptism is a child's introduction into the religious community, it is usually performed within the community at regular Sunday mass. Thus, it's not uncommon during mass for there to be a number

of children (from infants to ten-year-olds) waiting
to be christened after the regular service. Baptisms
are a smaller affair than weddings, usually restricted
to family and close friends, but also involve a large
meal afterward. It is also customary to take a gift for
the child, usually a piece of silverwork with religious
significance, such as a cross pendant or a medallion
portraying a saint.

Funerals

Funerals are solemn affairs and don't involve eating
or drinking. A death is usually announced by the
family in a local newspaper, along with the time
and place of the funeral service for those wishing
to pay their respects and attend services. People
who want to offer their condolences may do so at
the wake before the religious ceremony, and many
churches and chapels place an attendance book in the
entrance for those wishing to sign, as well as a plate
to leave personal cards. Once the service has ended,
attendants will follow the casket on foot (if a short
distance) or drive to the cemetery for the burial or
cremation, after which people go their separate ways.
Women wear black or white for funerals, while men
wear suits and a black tie. One week after the death, a
seventh-day mass is held to pray for the deceased and
for people once again to offer their condolences and
pay their respects.

Fado musicians stir heart strings in Lisbon.

FADO

The precise origins of *fado* are unclear, but on one point everyone agrees: these quintessentially Portuguese melodies are the true expression of the Portuguese soul. The word "*fado*" derives from the Latin "*fatum*," which means fate. The songs, melancholic lamentations accompanied by the Portuguese guitar, mirror the Portuguese romantic and fatalistic side, describing the pain and *saudade* of surrendering to one's destiny.

One theory states that *fado* descends from Moorish chants, which were also melancholic and doleful. Others suggest that the songs came from the medieval jesters and troubadours who sang about friendship and love as well as criticizing politics and society through satire. The most common explanation, however, is that *fado* derives from "*lundum*," the music sung by Brazilian slaves, and was brought to Lisbon in the mid-nineteenth century by Portuguese sailors. The first known *fado* songs speak of the sea and distant lands and therefore seem to support this theory.

The Portuguese guitar is one of *fado*'s main symbols, the other being the black shawl. Men usually sing *fado* wearing a dark suit, while women are also dressed in dark colors with a black shawl draped over one or both shoulders. Themes usually revolve around the pain of love and/or death, though individual songs can broach any subject from horses and bullfights to politics and patriotism. "Typical" *fado* is sung in small, dark restaurants and taverns in the older parts of Lisbon such as Alfama and the Bairro Alto, and the artists can be the most unlikely people, even one of the waiters serving tables. Though conversation can flow normally when no one is performing, it is important to keep quiet when someone is singing or the singer and fellow patrons may take offense. Of course, with artists like Amália Rodrigues, Dulce Pontes, and Marisa, *fado* has reached an international audience and, thanks to the recordings of new artists like Carminho and Ana Moura, can also be enjoyed at home or in a more modern setting.

In Coimbra, the *fado* tradition took a slightly different direction. Coimbra housed the country's first university, and young people from Lisbon and Porto would flock there to receive their education, taking along their guitars and their songs and instilling *fado* in the student community. Little could better impress a young woman than a suitor standing under her window at night serenading her with heart-wrenching songs of unrequited love. Nor could any other music better explain the *saudade* of leaving behind the best years of one's youth and the bohemian student life. Thus *fado* became the official anthem for graduating university students. Toward the end of the academic year, groups of students from universities around the country can still be seen wandering the city streets at night in their thick black cloaks, playing their guitars and singing their serenades.

RIBBON-BURNING

The ribbon-burning tradition (*queima das fitas*) carried out by graduating university students, mainly in the north of Portugal, dates back to the mid-nineteenth century. Upon finishing their exams,

Graduates in Porto celebrate at the *queima das fitas* procession.

students would group together by faculty and form a procession from the university to the town or city's main square, where they would burn the ribbons used to tie their books together. Over the years, this tradition has grown in participation and sophistication, and there is now an official ribbon-burning week in May, with organized activities and festivities.

This week usually begins with a monumental serenade where the academic community comes together to sing *fado* and other songs. At these concerts, rather than clapping, the students shake their satchels, displaying all their ribbons, which are covered with signatures of professors, colleagues, friends, and family. There is also usually a religious ceremony where the ribbons and satchels are blessed. After this, the week continues with sketches that parody the professors and academic life, processions, and large parties and concerts. In Porto and Coimbra, ribbon-burning week is a major event, with the activities and events usually making the front pages of the newspapers.

BULLFIGHTING

Drawings found in caves throughout the Iberian Peninsula suggest that the ritualistic relationship between man and bull dates back to prehistory. The practice of letting bulls loose among crowds for amusement began during the summer fairs and festivals of the Middle Ages. The art of bullfighting on horseback as it is seen today was developed as entertainment for the aristocracy in the sixteenth century. Later came the practice of bullfighting on foot, which brought the tradition to the masses. Bullfighting in Portugal is of extreme cultural importance; the Portuguese pride themselves on the rituals and traditions of what is considered an art form, and the *toureiros* (bullfighters) are regarded as heroes for their skill and bravery.

Bullfighting season begins on Easter Sunday and runs through to October. There are *corridas* (races) or *touradas* (bullfights) throughout the country on most weekends, every Thursday night in Lisbon during the summer months, and every day during the weeklong rural fairs that take place in the Ribatejo. The Ribatejo is the region northeast of Lisbon where the bullfighting tradition is strongest and where most of the bulls are bred. In each *corrida,* six or eight bulls are fought one at a time, with approximately half an hour allocated to each bull. The number of bullfighters varies between one and four, with each bullfighter usually facing two or three bulls. The *toureiro* performs either on horseback or on foot, never doing both. The bullfights themselves can be on foot, on horseback, or a variation of the two.

Bullfights follow a rigid set of rules and the fighters themselves are very superstitious, each with their own personal rituals for preparing for the fight. Once in the ring, the first part of the spectacle involves bullfighters on horseback dominating the bull with lances, while the matadors on foot show their skill leading the bull with a crimson cloak. For *corridas* on foot, the next phase is for the *banderilheiros* to face the bull head-on and stick pairs of small spears in its back, ending once again with the matador and his dance with the red cape. With *touradas* on horseback, the show is brought to a close with the *pega,* where a group of eight *forcados* literally take the bull by the horns and tail and bring it to a standstill with their bare hands. A band plays *paso dobles* and other traditional bullfighting music to accompany the performance, and there is a trumpeter, who stands and plays certain notes to signal changes in the program. Bullfights are not for the squeamish, but observing the enthusiasm and appreciation shown by the crowd as they applaud, throw flowers, handkerchiefs, and even items of clothing is a spectacle in itself.

Unlike in Spain, in Portugal the bull is not killed in the ring. At the end of each round, it is led out by a herd of cows to be slaughtered for beef. Modern proponents of the tradition will explain that the bulls used are raised specifically for bullfighting and are treated well during their lives. However, today, more and more view it as a cruel and inhumane practice, and an increasing number argue that it is time to end the custom. While the future of bullfighting in Portugal is uncertain, one thing is clear: this centuries-old tradition continues to provoke strong emotions on both sides of the debate.

Toureiros in traditional costume size up their match.

CHAPTER FOUR

MAKING FRIENDS

With friendship being such a closed and family-oriented affair in Portugal, newcomers may find people somewhat aloof and standoffish at first. In general, the Portuguese are wary of the unfamiliar, be it people or situations, so newcomers can often find themselves greeted with a certain amount of reservation. Don't let this put you off, however. Once you've learned to respect the boundaries and principles outlined in this chapter, and have been accepted into their circle, you will find your efforts well rewarded with firm and loyal friendships that last a lifetime.

CLOSE-KNIT CIRCLES

Because they tend to keep company mostly with family or close friends they have known since childhood or adolescence, the Portuguese can seem suspicious of strangers. Once the ice is broken, however, and they feel assured there is no hidden agenda, they become affectionate and helpful, so if properly approached are easily won over.

Friendships in Portugal are nurtured and cherished; maintaining regular contact is key as it indicates that you're willing to make an effort. When talking to someone, whether in person or on the phone, it's important to begin by inquiring about their and their family's general well-being before getting down to something more specific. Asking about a person's health is always a good start as the Portuguese can be quite fond of describing symptoms, ailments, medical consultations, and diagnostics in great detail to someone who's willing to listen.

In Portugal, communities are small, independent worlds where everyone knows everyone. Having a friend or acquaintance in common thus makes it easier for others to place and accept you. If you want to meet local people, use the neighborhood shops and become a regular in local cafés and taverns, so that people will begin to recognize and acknowledge you. It's likely that you'll feel observed and talked about at first, but don't feel uncomfortable. The Portuguese do this openly without disguising the fact that they're making comments about someone in their presence. If you maintain an open and friendly demeanor, their assessment of you will be positive. Offering to help with something they may need is also a sure way of being accepted. Don't forget, manners are highly regarded in Portugal and until a certain level of intimacy is reached, as a sign of respect, treat others with some formality.

INVITATIONS HOME

The Portuguese love to entertain at home and if they think someone is on their own, are quick to extend an invitation. They are proud of their local and family traditions and are eager to share these with guests who they hope will enjoy and be impressed by what's offered. Be sure to try the food offered, even if it seems unappetizing, since chances are it's a family recipe or something *típico*. It's important to your hosts that you feel welcome and comfortable, so there's no need to be overly formal as someone's guest. By all means arrive casually dressed, but be sure to be presentable and groomed.

While invitations are made out of genuine friendship and empathy, it's generally expected that the gesture will be reciprocated, either at home or a restaurant. Be sure to phone or to send a message within the following few days to say thank you; this indicates not only gratitude for the courtesy offered but also a willingness to maintain contact.

GIFT GIVING

When visiting someone's home, be sure to greet everyone in the household, and on the first visit bring your host or hostess a gift. Red wine, chocolate, pastries, or flowers are all good options. (Don't give carnations, however, as these carry a political meaning: red carnations in particular are the symbol of the revolutionary coup that took place in 1974.) There is a saying in Portuguese that "he who kisses my children sweetens my mouth," so if you are in doubt as to what to bring and your hosts have small children, taking a gift for the children is a good alternative.

SPORTS CLUBS

With such a mild climate, Portugal is ideal for outdoor sports such as golf, tennis, or sailing. When someone practices one of these, it's common for the whole family to meet at the club on the weekend for lunch or to spend the day. By becoming a member of one such club, you're far more likely to meet people with common interests. When in their clubs, people tend to be more at ease and ready to socialize with strangers. Attending regularly helps build familiarity, too. Gyms are also a good place to meet people and there are plenty around. Both clubs and gyms generally require a membership fee followed by monthly or annual payments.

For those near the coast, surfing and kitesurfing have seen a major boom in Portugal in recent years and are extremely popular among people of every age, at every level. It's common to see adults changing out of their wetsuits and into their work clothes in their cars to get back to the office after a lunchtime surfing session or lesson. Most surf schools have facilities set up on the beaches, making this a good way not only to get started in the sport but also to meet people and make friends. Transportation can be provided for children to and from school

Soon-to-be surfers on a dry run. (Second from left has a long way to go!)

or home, making this an extremely convenient extracurricular activity, too.

Another sport that has taken off in Portugal recently and that offers opportunities for social interaction is padel tennis. The game is similar to tennis but played with four players and on a smaller court. Due to its popularity, most tennis clubs have now added padel courts to their site, in addition to the many padel clubs that have mushroomed around the country. Sessions and tournaments are typically open to all levels of players, so you don't need to be a pro to participate. And even if you aren't very good, you'll still have a lot of fun. So, if you'd like to meet new people without too much focus on athletic proficiency, finding somewhere to play paddle ball is certainly worth a go.

EXPATRIATE CLUBS

The best way to blend in and get to know Portuguese culture is to mix with the locals, and for that there is no substitute. Along the way, however, it can be invaluable to connect with others from your national or cultural background, particularly if you're planning on staying in Portugal for any significant period of time.

Expatriate clubs can be found in Portugal's main cities and are helpful for both meeting those who have gone through the process of cultural acclimation themselves and for sourcing practical information on settling down. In Porto, for example, the port wine industry has created a sizeable British community. Aside from the British, there are also many German, Dutch, and South African immigrants who have settled along the beautiful Estoril coast, just west of Lisbon, and, of course, in the Algarve. The best way to obtain information about expatriate clubs is online, including on Facebook, as well as through consulates and embassies.

English-language Publications

There are two main English-language newspapers published in Portugal: the *Portugal News* is weekly and has national coverage and distribution as well as an online edition (www.theportugalnews.com). The *Portugal Resident* has a daily online publication (www.portugalresident.com) and three weekly regional editions focusing on the Algarve, greater Lisbon area, and Madeira. Major international newspapers and magazines are widely available.

DOS AND DON'TS

While most will overlook the unwitting faux pas of foreign visitors, there are a few pointers on etiquette that are worth keeping in mind if you want to make a good impression:

- Avoid stretching or sprawling out in public places, and keep your feet off furniture.
- Don't turn your back to someone you're in a group with; if it's unavoidable, excuse yourself beforehand.
- At the table, hold your knife in your right hand and use it to push the food onto your fork, which remains in your left hand. The North American habit of cutting the food first and then eating using only the fork in the right hand is considered bad manners.
- When eating, try to maintain good posture; keep both hands above the table and your napkin on your lap.
- Food like shellfish can be eaten with your fingers, but don't lick them!
- If you're unsure whether a dish is finger food, follow your host's example.
- When you've finished eating, place your knife and fork next to each other on the plate.
- Smoking used to be very common in Portugal;

however, anti-smoking legislation passed in 2014 made it illegal to smoke in all bars, restaurants, and nightclubs. This, in addition to regular increases in tobacco tax, led many to quit the habit. Electric cigarettes and vaping, meanwhile, have become popular. While there are currently no specific laws regulating their use, there is a consensus that they should be used in the same way as regular cigarettes, i.e. not in enclosed public spaces or around children.

CHAPTER FIVE

AT HOME

PORTUGUESE HOMES

In the main cities and towns, most Portuguese live in apartments. These can vary from modest two-bedroom, one-bathroom homes in large apartment complexes to spacious five-bedroom flats in luxury condominiums with communal garden and pool areas. Away from the urban centers, townhouses and villas (*vivendas*) with ground-level patios or gardens become more numerous. Due to rent laws that heavily favored the tenant over the landlord and made evicting difficult tenants a long and complicated process that most owners were not willing to risk, most homes used to be owned rather than rented. However, amendments made to the Urban Lease Law in 2012 enabling owners to update their rents and facilitate the eviction process has resulted in a new and very dynamic rental market.

Added to this, the lack of mortgage lending brought about by the economic crisis has also forced many Portuguese to rent rather than buy their residences.

A range of tax benefits implemented to attract foreign investment and encourage property refurbishment (such as Golden Visas, the Non-Habitual Residents Tax Regime, and incentives to Urban Regeneration) have also increased demand,

Traditional apartment buildings in downtown Lisbon.

and have had particular impact on the rental sector. These measures, along with the rise in tourism, have created a wave of urban regeneration in city centers and a new trend in short-term rental that has transformed the property market. Property prices have risen as a result, and as such, young Portuguese on low starting salaries are generally restricted to renting, often sharing apartments with friends in order to save enough money to buy their own home down the line.

Apartments and houses vary in degrees of comfort and charm according to age. The interest of foreign and national investment to renovate and renew Portugal's major cities has transformed once drafty and uncomfortable, but charming, old buildings into comfortable dwellings fitted with modern comforts such as quality materials and central heating. The materials used depend on the region. In the north, more angular houses made primarily of stone and wood predominate, while in the south, rounded, whitewashed, Moorish-looking architecture is more common. Traditional colorful Portuguese tiles are widely used all over the country, especially in bathrooms and kitchens, and on facades. Newly built homes are more comfortable and follow a streamlined, more minimalist vein, using modern materials, and are equipped with central heating and better insulation.

Rural houses on the Cávado River, in the northwestern Entre Douro e Minho region.

Due to urban centers being cramped and crowded, many people have a second home in the country or on the coast for weekends and vacations. These can range from a plot of land with a spacious home that provides escape from the small quarters of a city apartment, to an even smaller apartment on the coast, but with ocean views and a beach nearby. Those who do not have an alternative, but come to the city for work, may choose to spend weekends and vacations in their hometowns with extended families.

Beware of weekend traffic because people who have the option prefer to flee the city whenever they can, especially on public holidays or in the summer, when the downtown heat is stifling.

THE HOUSEHOLD

Housewife in Portuguese is *dona de casa*, which can be translated literally as "owner or lady of the house." Traditionally, the father was considered the head of the family, but it was the mother who ran the home and carried most of the domestic responsibility, often in addition to working. Nowadays, thanks to greater equality and women becoming an integral part of corporate workplaces, women and men more equally share household and family responsibilities. Both will take an active role in their children's lives, and when it comes to making a family decision, everyone has a say.

Portuguese women may spend considerably less time at home than they once used to, but they are still extremely house-proud and make a point of having a spotless and well-organized home. When visiting other homes, they will notice if they are clean and tidy and may well make a comment if someone's house falls short of their standards (though not necessarily in the person's presence!). Aside from an eye for cleanliness, meals are usually cooked fresh every day and from scratch, since anything preprepared or frozen is frowned upon.

Aunties and In-Laws

After returning from their honeymoon and setting up house, newlywed couples are expected to host their respective families. Whether they've invited the whole family at once or a few at a time, the young couple will have to rise to the occasion, which generally means preparing for their female relatives and in-laws to leave no stone unturned. A complete tour of the new home must be given, and drawers, closets, and cabinets will be inspected and scrutinized!

Diet varies from region to region, but most meals begin with soup, followed by a meat, fish, or poultry dish with rice or potatoes, and fruit for dessert. Fresh produce in Portugal is of excellent quality and requires little preparation, but the Portuguese also love heavier dishes stewed in olive oil or tomato-based sauces.

Breakfast and dinner are family affairs, with everyone eating together whenever possible. Breakfast is usually a light meal of bread, coffee, and milk, while dinner is heavier and considered the main family meal of the day. In the north, many families also come home from work and school for lunch; this is less common further south. Working parents usually shop for groceries at the end of the day and prepare dinner when they get home, with the evening meal taking place at around 8:00 p.m. Toddlers generally eat earlier, and in this case parents may choose to have dinner after putting them to bed. Children seldom help around the house, although this is changing, and they are increasingly given chores to help parents who work long hours and have less time to dedicate to cooking and cleaning.

SHOPPING

The shopping center boom in the early 1990s brought with it the hypermarket trend. These large supermarkets are usually found in shopping malls and have everything

Locals shop for produce at the market in Cascais.

from food and household products to clothes and sporting goods. Low prices and long working hours (usually from around 9:00 a.m. to 10:00 p.m.) make these stores very popular for monthly or weekly shopping at night or on the weekend.

For fresh produce and daily staples, people still prefer their neighborhood shops. Bread is usually bought from the bakery every morning. Fruit and vegetables come from the local *mercearia*, a small grocer, or from the municipal market (*mercado*), which is open every day except Monday from around 8:00 a.m. to 1:00 p.m. Once a week most municipalities also have an open-air market, the *feira*, that runs from early morning to lunchtime, with gypsies and traders selling clothes, accessories, kitchen utensils, baked goods, and fresh food. Every neighborhood has at least one pharmacy, and these take weekly turns running a twenty-four-hour shift. The name and address of the establishment providing a night service is posted on all pharmacy windows and is also available online at www.farmaciasdeservico.net. Small shops and pharmacies run from around 9:00 a.m. to 6:00 or 7:00 p.m. and may close for up to two hours at lunchtime. Banking hours are usually from 8:30 a.m. to 3:00 p.m.; some branches, however, are open from 10:00 a.m. to 5:00 p.m. There is a large network of ATM machines (*multibanco*) that allow one not only to withdraw and deposit funds, but also to pay bills and taxes, transfer money, and even purchase train tickets.

MONEY

Online shopping has become very popular in Portugal in recent years for everything from fashion and homeware to supermarket groceries for home delivery. In general, older people will still carry cash for smaller sums, while younger Portuguese prefer to go cashless and are happy to rely almost entirely on electronic payment methods. A popular payment app in Portugal is MB WAY (MB stands for *multibanco*, or ATM). This cell phone app is used for shop payments, for transferring money between friends and to pay for services, and to generate codes that can be used to withdraw money at an ATM machine, making this a convenient way for parents to send their children funds remotely. Cheques in Portugal have become almost obsolete, except for very specific situations involving large sums.

DAILY LIFE

In Portuguese homes the day usually begins with family breakfast at around 8:00 a.m., after which children are taken to school and parents go to work. During the workday plenty of coffee breaks are taken. The first one takes place on arriving to the office, with colleagues, among plenty of noise and activity at a nearby café. Another coffee is generally shared mid-morning, followed by a lunch break at around 1:00 p.m., which lasts around an hour and a half. There may be another coffee break mid-afternoon, with the day ending somewhere between 5:30 and 7:00 p.m. It's important to note that punctuality is not a Portuguese virtue and as such it's common for people to be flexible with their working hours, starting and ending later than expected.

Once the workday has ended, most people head home. In the summer months, when daylight lasts until around 9:00 p.m., groups often get together for a drink on an esplanade at the end of the day, and children might be taken to the park or the beach.

Many urban centers lie on the coast and the waterfront areas are well designed for leisure and activities. Either before or after dinner many families will make the most of the pleasant evenings and enjoy these areas on foot or bicycles. The Portuguese also love to socialize and go out, so restaurants and bars pick up the pace as early as Wednesday or Thursday, staying open until well after midnight.

Friends enjoy coffee and cake in a Porto café.

COFFEE CULTURE

Any excuse is a good excuse for a coffee break
in Portugal, where for the enthusiastic, life is
punctuated by up to five or six cups throughout the
day. People are happy to enjoy their coffee at home, at
the office, or in a café, many of which are busy all day
and where the din around breakfast and lunchtime
can make normal conversation almost impossible. In
general, the coffee in Portugal is of excellent quality.
The main local brands are Nicola, Torrié, Sical, and
Delta, the latter two holding by far the largest market
share. These firms import the beans from Africa
and South America to then grind and roast the

coffee domestically. Foreign brands such as Buondi, Segafredo, and Lavazza are also widely available, and most homes have a capsule coffee machine, such as Nespresso or other supermarket brands.

When it comes to ordering your coffee, there are a few things to keep in mind. If you order a *café* you'll receive a regular espresso in a small porcelain cup, but there are a number of terms the locals use to state their preference. For instance, in Lisbon, a *bica* (pronounced "beeka") is also a term used to request a regular coffee, while in the north the locals may ask for a *cimbalino*, a word that derives from Cimbali, an Italian brand of espresso machines used in many establishments.

A *café curto* (literally meaning "short coffee") means the person wants their cup less full than a regular coffee, while an *italiana* is even shorter and very concentrated. A *café comprido* (literally "long coffee") is almost full to the brim, and can also be called *café cheio*, which means "full coffee."

Then there is the *carioca*, which is a weaker coffee made by watering the grain down slightly. For this, a normal coffee has to be taken first and then the *carioca* is made, using the same blend from the previous coffee. Then there is what northerners call a *pingo,* literally meaning "a drop," which is a regular coffee with a drop of milk in it. In Lisbon, this is called a *garoto* (the literal translation of which is "little boy").

The Portuguese version of *café au lait* is called a *galão,* which is served in a tall glass, or a *meia de leite*, which literally translated means "half of milk," which is served in a mug. However, foreigners need not balk at this complex "Javanese"; if you simply order a *café,* you'll be given a regular espresso, and if it's a traditional *café au lait* you'd like, ask for a *café com leite* (pronounced "late"). The above-mentioned varieties are also all available in decaffeinated versions—in Portuguese, *descafeinado*.

TELEVISION

Television is extremely popular in Portugal and the TV set is often on for as long as there are people at home. The most popular programs are the news broadcasts, the beloved national and Brazilian soap operas, and reality shows. The soap operas (*novelas*) compete for television ratings with live soccer broadcasts and reality or talent shows such as "The Voice," which are followed religiously and are hot topics of conversation in the cafés in the morning. There are also a wide range of international channels and digital streaming services available, both of which are offered by Portugal's main Internet companies (Meo, Nos, and Vodafone). For more on TV and Internet, see Chapter 9.

CHILDREN

Children are the center of the family, and from an early age accompany their parents everywhere, from restaurants and hotels to shopping malls and sometimes the office. Yet, like everything else in Portuguese society, their upbringing is at times boisterous and contradictory. Adults may be seen scolding children loudly and spanking them in public one moment, then hugging them vigorously and smothering them with kisses the next. Children are expected to abide by strict rules of behavior, but then are indulged with material things, which they soon get a taste for.

Children in Portugal today are typically raised by both parents, though they'll often rely on help from the grandparents who are viewed as surrogate parents and have full authority over the children. Mothers are fiercely protective of their offspring and will not tolerate any form of aggression toward their child from other children or other adults. Public day care is available from the age of four months but where possible, parents prefer to leave their children at home with a family member or caretaker until they're around three years old which is when they can attend preschool.

As in many countries around the world with a growing middle class, parents will often have a more open and realistic attitude toward their teenage children than in the past, although girls are still urged to guard their "reputation." Sexual education is taught in school from grade eight and many families are adopting a more open attitude toward sexuality. That said, in many households, parents are still uncomfortable discussing the topic.

In the past, children were only expected to leave home when they married. Today, however, many leave home to attend university and as young professionals prefer to rent an apartment while concentrating on their careers before settling down and starting a family. There is also greater acceptance of couples living together outside of wedlock. As a result, the average marriage age in Portugal has risen steadily and in 2021 was 39 for men and 36.5 for women, according to the National Institute for Statistics.

EDUCATION

The education system in Portugal used to be of poor quality in comparison with the rest of Europe. It was fairly common for Portuguese students to fail regularly and drag out their secondary and higher education over a number of years. This has improved in recent decades, however, and progress is visible at both secondary and university level.

School attendance is mandatory between the ages of six and eighteen, though, as mentioned, many children will attend preschool from age three and sometimes earlier. Secondary education (from the age of fifteen) is mandatory. Public school fees are means-tested and set according to the family's income. For those who can afford them, there are also a large number of private and international schools.

The school year lasts from September to June, and a normal school day is a long one. Classes start between 8:30 and 9:00 a.m. and often run until 4:00 or 5:00 p.m. After classes, many children go on to various extracurricular activities.

Students at the University of Coimbra. Built in 1290, the university is one of the world's oldest and is a UNESCO World Heritage Site.

There are numerous public and private universities in Portugal as well as many polytechnical institutes. Students who apply for higher education must complete a national (for public institutions) or local (for private institutions) entrance exam to qualify. More than 20 percent of the student population continue on to higher education, and the Portuguese government committed to create incentives to increase this number significantly in its Portugal 2020 program. Approximately 40,000 educational grants were awarded in that year alone and enrollment continues to rise.

BUREAUCRACY

Obtaining even the most basic official documents
in Portugal used to be an extremely lengthy and
bureaucratic process. Lines were interminable,
numerous photocopies and photographs were
necessary, and a long wait before receiving the final
document was guaranteed. People love to complain
about the complication and tedium involved in
the bureaucratic process, but do nothing about it
and sometimes use a two-hour wait as an excuse to
avoid going back to work. Though long waits can
still be expected at the different government offices,
for certain simpler matters, such as renewing a
passport or driver's license, the government has
opened a "one-stop shop" in most of the bigger
cities. These "*Lojas do Cidadão*," which literally
means "citizens' shop," usually speed up the process
greatly. It is also now possible to take care of many
bureaucratic services online, with relatively easy
and efficient Web sites to manage everything from
taxes to social security. Still, these are mostly only
available in Portuguese, so be prepared to fill out
many forms and to return more than once before
all the necessary information is imparted. Patience
is key, and if you can find a local friend to help
you, all the better.

MILITARY SERVICE

Military service was compulsory in Portugal until 2004, when the armed forces were made fully professional. Nowadays young men are no longer obliged to participate in military training, but conscription for both men and women is implemented if insufficient people volunteer. All citizens do receive a call notice from the Ministry of Defense on the year they turn eighteen to attend National Defense Day, a mandatory full-day information session on national defense.

Changing of the Guard at Belém Palace, the official residence of the Portuguese president in Lisbon.

CHAPTER SIX

TIME OUT

The Portuguese live for family gatherings and social occasions. Opportunities to get together with friends and family are taken advantage of and relished. Food is taken very seriously—people are often willing to make a day or weekend trip just to savor a local delicacy—and it often plays a central role at social gatherings. Meals in general are very social affairs, where sharing experiences and conversation is just as important as enjoying the food.

The Portuguese are fashion conscious and like to dress for the occasion. Women in particular take great care in their appearance, will dress stylishly and be up to date on the latest trends—one may only be leaving the house to pick up groceries, but that doesn't mean one shouldn't be well groomed! Indeed, even gym outfits will be planned with care. Visitors should pack accordingly.

FOOD

Food in Portugal is steeped in history and tradition.
Irrigation and gardening techniques dating back
to Moorish times created the olive groves and
vineyards that provide the ingredients at the center
of the Portuguese diet. Vasco da Gama's discovery
of the maritime route to the Far East brought a
wide variety of spices that are still staples in every
Portuguese kitchen, such as coriander, pepper,
and paprika. The exploration of Africa and South
America supplied the peppers, potatoes, vegetables,
fruit, and coffee essential to most dishes and meals.

Seafood

The cold waters of the Atlantic provide a wealth
of seafood, and Portugal's fish and shellfish are
considered among the world's tastiest. One of the
least expensive and most widely enjoyed fresh
fish is the sardine, which can be seen and smelled
grilling on barbecues all summer long and is the
main feature on the *Santos Populares* menu. Grilled
sardines are eaten plain with just olive oil drizzled
over them, or on top of a chunk of fresh bread, with
boiled potatoes and marinated roasted peppers as
side dishes.

Dried, salted codfish is a regular several times
a week in every Portuguese home. There are

Grilled sardines garnished with garlic and fresh lemon and served with a fresh tomato salad.

supposedly as many ways to cook cod (*bacalhau*) as there are days in the year, and most families have their own favorite cod recipe that has been passed down from previous generations.

Shellfish is also popular, with dishes such as stuffed crab, hot or cold mussels (*mexilhões*), and clams (*ameijoas*) stewed in a variety of ways, always with plenty of garlic and fresh coriander.

There are also many freshwater fish, such as the lamprey (*lampreia*) from the Minho region, which is considered a delicacy and is available only in the spring. The warmer waters of the Azores and Madeira provide their own species of seafood, such as *lapas*—crustaceans that cling to rocks—as well as all the traditional fresh fish, tuna being a favorite.

Meat Dishes

The Portuguese are very fond of meat, fowl, and game, with recipes varying according to each region's local traditions. Smoked ham (*presunto*) and spicy *chouriço* sausages are everywhere. From the north come further delicacies such as roast lamb and suckling pig, as well as smoked pork, various sausages, and tripe dishes. Pork is also very popular in the Alentejo, where wheat abounds, along with olive and cork trees that release nuts and truffles for the pigs to enjoy.

All over the country, each region has its own version of *favas* and *feijoada*, two rich, aromatic stewed dishes comprised of beans and a variety of fresh and smoked meats. There is also the *cozido à Portuguesa*, where beef and pork are stewed in the same pot as a series of vegetables and herbs, again with individual regions adding their local touches. The year-round mild climate in the Azores and Madeira provides prime conditions for cattle to graze and a wide array of tropical fruits and vegetables to grow. Beef is tender and of excellent quality, and the local yams and cornbread are a must at every meal.

Mock Pork Sausages

One of Portugal's delicacies, produced mainly in the Trás-os-Montes region, is *alheira*, a smoked sausage fried in oil or baked in the oven and served with leafy greens, homemade fries, and fried egg—not exactly a light meal! The story behind these sausages dates back to the Inquisition, when Jews would make them with poultry flesh and fat, bread, garlic, and spices, and hang them in the window so that when the Inquisitors passed, they would assume the *alheiras* were regular pork sausages belonging to a non-Jewish household. *Alheira* is still a popular dish; however, the modern versions do contain pork.

Soups

Soup is usually a part of lunch and dinner in Portuguese homes. Hot or cold soups are very popular in the Alentejo, and are substantial enough to serve as a main course, often including bread, beans, poached eggs, or even fish and meat.

Stone soup (*sopa da pedra*), which is a specialty of the Ribatejo region, is a rich, thick soup made from an assortment of beans, pork, *chouriço* sausage, vegetables, and spices.

Stone Soup

The fable of stone soup was written by Teofilo Braga (1843–1924), a popular Portuguese writer and politician. The story tells of a monk who was begging from door to door. Starving and having received nothing from yet another household, he looked to the ground and picked up a stone, cleaned it off, and claimed he would make stone broth. When the family laughed at him, he feigned surprise and informed them that the dish was very tasty. Curious, the family said they wanted to watch him make it, so the monk asked them for a pot, into which he placed the stone and then filled with water. He then asked them to place the pot on their stove in order for the water to boil. Once the water had boiled, the monk asked for some lard, followed by salt, *chouriço*, and bread, all of which they gave him. When he had finished eating the soup, the family asked the monk about the stone at the bottom of the pot, to which he replied that he would be taking it with him for next time.

Hearty slow-cooked *sopa da pedra* served with a crusty loaf.

Chicken *Piri-piri*

A healthier and tastier alternative to fast food in
Portugal is chicken *piri-piri*, or *frango no churrasco*,
which translated literally is barbecued chicken. *Piri-
piri* is a hot sauce, but this chicken, found mainly in
the greater Lisbon area, is available in both hot and
non-spicy versions. Whole chickens are cut down
the middle and placed spread-eagle on a spit over a
coal barbecue. A chicken is removed from the spit to
order, and is then brushed with either hot butter or a
spicy sauce, whichever the customer prefers. In some

Chicken *piri-piri*: a popular and delicious fast food alternative.

of these establishments, you can sit at a table and
eat your chicken there, while others offer a take-out
service only.

Cheese

From sheep, goat, and cow's milk come an impressive
variety of Portuguese cheeses. The textures vary from
rich and creamy to drier, harder cheeses, and flavors
range from delicate and mild to extremely strong.
Some cheeses are served as appetizers while others
come after a meal with port or red wine. Like the
traditional dishes, cheeses also change from region
to region, with the buttery *queijo da serra* produced
in the north, Serpa cheese from the Alentejo, and the
parmesan-like *queijo da ilha* from the Azores.

Ovos moles: a sweet egg paste-filled delicacy from the city of Aveiro.

Pastel de nata: rich baked custard in a crisp buttery puff pastry.

Desserts

The Portuguese also have an extremely sweet tooth. In the seventeenth and eighteenth centuries, convents made their pastries famous by competing with each other to see who could produce the most divine desserts. This resulted in extremely delicate and rich cakes, pies, and puddings with very allusive names, such as *barriga de freira* ("nun's belly"), *toucinho do ceu* ("heaven's lard"), and *pudim de abade de priscos* ("abbot's pudding"). From the Algarve come delicate marzipan desserts shaped like fruit, fish, or seashells. Sweet egg paste is used in many desserts such as Aveiro's *ovos moles* (soft eggs) as well as the burnt custard seen in the famous Belém *pastel de nata* (cream pastry), whose recipe is still a well-guarded secret today.

WINE

Portugal has been exporting its wine since the Middle Ages and has come to occupy an important position in today's international wine markets. With such an extensive variety, commercial wine production is heavily regulated and classified according to geographic origins and specific characteristics, with every phase of production under strict control. The wine regions, officially known as *regiões demarcadas* (demarcated regions), indicate the wine's geographic origin as well as the attributes particular to that area.

Portuguese wines can be placed into two broad categories: VQPRD, which means Quality Wine Produced in a Determined Region, and Table wines. Bottles bearing the VQPRD seal contain quality wines produced in a specific demarcated region. In each region, local commissions regulate the production and classify the VQPRD wines as DOC (Denomination of Controlled Origin) or Regional.

DOC wines are produced in limited quantities and must follow strict rules of production regarding the variety, selection, geographic origin of the grapes, alcohol content, and specific vinification processes. They must also conform to certain standards of clarity, aroma, and flavor. Regional wines are local wines produced in a specified region, but which do not follow the same strict rules of production as DOC wines.

Table wines are considered of lesser quality, do not have a geographic demarcation, and are not permitted to mention grape variety or the year of harvest on the label.

Vinho verde ("green wine"), a light, slightly sparkling wine ideal with seafood or just to cool down on a hot day, is produced only in Portugal along the Minho coast. Also in the north lies the Douro Valley, the oldest demarcated region in the world (since 1756), where some of the country's best full-bodied red wines are produced, as well as the world-renowned port wine. The valley can be visited by car, boat, or train and offers beautiful views of the wine family estates and terraced vineyards. Head downstream to Gaia, directly across the river from Porto, for wine tasting in the port wine cellars.

Toward the center of the country, vineyards run from the mountainous regions of the Dão and Bairrada to the flatter Ribatejo and Oeste (meaning west) region on the coast. Closer to Lisbon, the lush hills of Sintra produce the red wines of Colares, and toward Mafra lies Bucelas, which boasts some of the best Portuguese whites. Further south, the Costa Azul provides not only wonderful red and white wine but also the syrupy, sweet muscatel. In the south, the parched soils of the Alentejo and Algarve produce the fruity, apparently lighter wines that actually have an alcoholic content sometimes higher than 13 percent.

Madeira wine, the dessert wine that originates from that region, has always been very popular worldwide, especially in England. It is said that in the fifteenth century, when George, Duke of Clarence, was sentenced to death for plotting to overthrow his brother the king, Edward IV, he chose death by drowning in a butt of Malmsey—sweet Madeira wine.

These main regions offer eleven well-planned wine routes for those who wish to explore Portuguese wine culture and landscapes: the green wine route, the port wine route, the Cister vineyards route, the Dão wine route, the Bairrada wine route, the Beira Interior wine route, the west wine route, the Ribatejo vineyards route, the Bucelas, Carcavelos, and Colares wine routes, the Costa Azul wine route, and the Alentejo wine route. All offer visits of varying lengths with many interesting tourism and wine-related activities.

EATING OUT

The Portuguese enjoy nightlife, and this usually begins with dinner. Eating out takes place even later than when dining at home, with many establishments serving until as late as 11:00 p.m. or midnight. Restaurants vary greatly in sophistication and menus, so it's a good idea to ask a local for their suggestions, since a greasy-looking tavern (*tasca*) or grill

Alfresco dining on one of Lisbon's picturesque terraces.

(*churrasqueira*) can sometimes offer the best food in town. Most restaurants have menus in English and other languages, so be sure to ask. A lower-priced daily or tourist fixed menu (*ementa do dia* or *ementa turística*) consisting of an appetizer, main course, dessert, and a drink is also generally available and makes choosing easier.

Once you are seated, most restaurants will place bread, butter, olives, cheese, or some other variety of appetizers on the table. This is included in the cover charge and serves mainly to ease the wait involved after ordering, since fresh food will only be cooked once orders are placed.

Vegetarian and vegan restaurants were once hard to come by but are now more common, thanks in large part to the boom in tourism and foreign expats. Local chefs are eager to experiment with global trends and add a Portuguese twist, while foreign chefs and restauranteurs have brought new concepts and ethnic flavors from abroad. Outside the large urban centers, a wide variety of fresh vegetables and fish, as well as plenty of Italian and Asian restaurants, usually provides a tasty, meat-free alternative.

NIGHTLIFE

The nightlife in Portugal's cities is vibrant, with plenty of bars and nightclubs, also referred to as

Nightlife in Lisbon's Chiado neighborhood.

"discotheques," to choose from. These don't fill until after dinnertime, and often only really pick up around 1:00 or 2:00 a.m., staying open until 5:00 a.m. or later. Many discos charge an entrance fee that usually includes one free drink; otherwise, minimum consumption (also usually one drink) is imposed. In most clubs, the customer is given a card on which all drinks are noted; payment is then taken at the exit, so it's important not to lose the card or the maximum possible fee will be charged. On the streets outside you'll usually find stalls selling food such as hamburgers and hotdogs, and the night can go on until early morning.

TIPPING

There is no set rule when it comes to tipping in restaurants in Portugal, and tips are not usually included in the bill. The Portuguese generally tip between 0 and 5 percent, but foreigners are expected to leave around 10 percent. It's not customary to tip in bars or cafés, and in taxis the price is usually just rounded up to the nearest euro.

SHOPPING FOR PLEASURE

On the weekend, the large shopping centers fill to the brim with entire families browsing, eating, and shopping the day away. These malls are open seven days a week from 10:00 a.m. to 11:00 p.m., or sometimes later, and offer a large selection of well-known national and international brands, food, and cinema.

For more traditional, open-air shopping, most downtown areas (*baixa*) have pedestrian-only cobblestone streets lined with shops and cafés. Here anything from major brands to "typical" Portuguese arts and crafts can be found. These shops also open at 10:00 a.m., some closing for lunch between 1:00 p.m. and 3:00 p.m. and then reopening until 7:00 p.m. On Saturdays, many smaller or local shops close for the day at 1:00 p.m. Government-regulated sales take place twice yearly, in January/February and August/September. Good buys for visitors in Portugal include clothes and shoes, tiles and ceramics, and wine.

BANKS

Portugal's currency was the *escudo* until 1999, when the country became one of the eleven founding members of the euro. Apart from exchange desks at airports, foreign currency must be changed through a

The Barcelos Cockerel

The Barcelos cockerel has become a popular Portuguese mascot and is a recurrent motif in local handicrafts. The legend that made the rooster famous begins with a mysterious crime in Barcelos that left the townspeople shaken and afraid. When a pilgrim from Galicia passed through the town, allegedly on his way to Santiago de Compostela, the locals were quick to arrest him and condemn him for the crime. Before his execution, the Spaniard asked to be taken before the judge to plead his innocence. He was admitted to the judge's residence where a banquet was about to take place. Pointing to a roasted rooster on the table, the condemned man claimed that should he be innocent, the cooked cockerel would crow as he was being hanged. Sure enough, as he was about to hang, the rooster stood up on the table and crowed! The Spaniard was immediately set free, returning to Barcelos years later to raise a monument honoring the Virgin Mary and Saint James.

bank. There are many in the city centers and are easily recognizable. Banking hours are from 8:30 a.m. to between 3:00 p.m. and 5:00 p.m., depending on the branch, and there's a large network of ATM machines available twenty-four hours a day. The main Portuguese banks are Caixa Geral de Depositos, Millennium BCP, and Novo Banco. Most banks today offer their customers online services and via their own app platforms, which has helped to save time that would otherwise be spent waiting in line.

SPORTS

Without a doubt, the most popular sport in Portugal is soccer. Each town has its own team and playing field, but the main rivals are Benfica (Lisbon), Sporting (Lisbon), and FC Porto. When a game takes place between any of these teams, the country comes to a standstill as everyone watches live or on television, and afterwards the winning team's fans will take to the streets to celebrate the victory. Though people are fiercely loyal to their teams, outbursts of violence are very rare. Fans may provoke each other, and the occasional skirmish may break out, but these situations usually subside without the need for police intervention.

Portuguese soccer teams and players are considered among the best in the world, with legends such as Eusebio, Figo, and Cristiano Ronaldo winning international recognition.

Hosting Euro 2004 put Portugal on the world soccer map, and the country rose to the occasion by improving urban infrastructures and building several large, state-of-the-art stadiums. When in 2016 Portugal won the UEFA championship for the first time in the thrilling final played in the Stade de France in Paris, a wave of national pride took hold of the country.

Cristiano Ronaldo, widely regarded as one of the greatest soccer players of all time.

Aside from soccer, water sports are widely popular, and Portugal's 497 miles (800 km) of coastline and mild weather make it an ideal location. The country's beaches, such as Guincho (near Estoril) and Ericeira (near Mafra), offer some of the best surfing, windsurfing, and kitesurfing conditions in Europe, and host international championships every year.

Yacht clubs all over the country are busy all year-round organizing sailing events for every class of boat, from the smaller Olympic classes such as Laser to large sailboats. In 2004 Portugal was one of the contenders to host the America's Cup regatta on the Lisbon coast, making it to the final decision stages but losing in the end to the Spanish town of Valencia. In 2007 the prestigious ISAF Sailing World Championship took place in Cascais, and Lisbon was the first stop in the 2011–2012 America's Cup World Series Regattas. More recently, Lisbon hosted the Tall Ships Races between 2016 and 2021, as well as the Volvo Ocean Race between 2016 and 2018.

Tennis courts can be found in most towns around the country. Resorts in the Algarve, Madeira, and Estoril offer tennis holidays, and every year the Portugal Open is included in the ATP World Tours calendar, attracting international players and fans. The global padel tennis craze has taken hold in Portugal, too (see page 94), and there are many clubs where one can enjoy the game throughout the country.

Portuguese golf courses are considered among the finest in Europe, and from 2014 Portugal was named the World's Best Golf Destination by the World Golf Awards for five consecutive years. The better-known courses are in the Algarve and Estoril area, but there is also a wide selection along the west coast and in the northern part of the country.

Many Portuguese people enjoy an early morning

or evening walk, run, or bike ride, and city dwellers can often be seen taking to the seaside promenades for this kind of activity. For longer strolls, you can visit one of the many nature reserves, such as Sintra, Peneda-Gerês, Montesinho, and Madeira, and enjoy the dense, green landscapes on foot or bicycle.

VACATIONS

Many businesses close for all or part of the month of August, and most Portuguese take this time for their vacations as well. Vacations are generally spent en masse with friends and family. Those who have second homes or are away from their hometowns take the opportunity to enjoy these spots at a more leisurely pace. For those who choose to get away and rent accommodation, once an adequate destination is found, it'll usually be revisited year after year.

Large Portuguese communities in France, Germany, Switzerland, and Canada bring about an influx of emigrants who return to their hometowns for their summer and Christmas vacations, as well as family members in Portugal who travel to those countries to visit loved ones living abroad. Another favorite holiday destination is Brazil, which provides a warm break from the damp and chilly Portuguese winters.

With such an inviting coastline, however, virtually

everyone takes to the Portuguese beaches for their summer vacations. In the north, the ocean is rougher and cold, and the climate is less predictable, with summer mornings that can be quite misty and chilly. In the south, warmer water, sunny skies, and high temperatures are guaranteed, making the Alentejo and Algarve beaches among the most popular. This popularity has rendered the Algarve extremely busy and crowded in the summer months. As an alternative, discerning visitors could head north to discover the cooler temperatures and charm of the Minho and Douro regions.

CULTURAL ACTIVITIES

In 1994, Lisbon was the European Union's Capital of Culture, followed by Porto in 2001, and Guimarães in 2012. Lisbon was selected to host Web Summit, the largest tech event in Europe, for the first time in 2016 and in 2018 the partnership with the city was extended, with the event scheduled to take place there every year until 2028. These events not only broaden the country's cultural horizons, but also raise awareness of Portuguese culture abroad. One of the following four Portuguese cities will also host the European Capital of Culture in 2027: Aveiro, Ponta Delgada (Azores), Braga, or Évora.

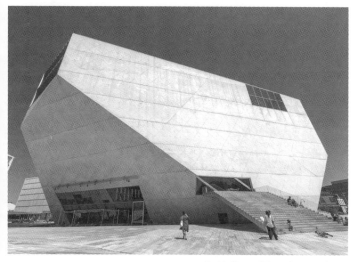

Porto's House of Music (Casa da Música).

The Museum of Art, Architecture, and Technology (MAAT) in Lisbon.

There are several well-respected foundations, such as the Gulbenkian in Lisbon and Serralves in Porto, which show the work of local artists and international touring companies. The Centro Cultural de Belém in Lisbon and the Casa da Música in Porto house impressive and modern auditoriums that offer a varied choice of national and foreign dance and music programs.

Pop culture is a favorite in Portugal and most major pop and rock artists pass through Lisbon or Porto or both, filling stadiums to capacity. The cinema is also very popular, with many Hollywood films making it to the Portuguese screens, playing in the original version with Portuguese subtitles. Portuguese cinema is of excellent quality but still relatively unknown, and of course there is the language barrier. Still, artists like Joaquim de Almeida, Maria de Medeiros, and Marisa Cruz have achieved international recognition, as did the film director Manoel de Oliveira, who was recognized with several international awards at prestigious events such as the Berlinale, Golden Globes, and Cannes Film Festival, and worked with celebrities like John Malkovich and Catherine Deneuve. In 2021 Netflix released its first Portuguese original series called *Glória*, an intense Cold War spy thriller set in 1960s Portugal.

The Glass Route

The Glass Route, in the Estremadura e Ribatejo region, aims to promote the area's rich glass manufacturing tradition. Five glass manufacturers and two museums have joined the Fatima/Leiria tourism board in this project to offer a tour of the area and display the history of Portuguese glasswork, which dates back to the beginning of the eighteenth century, as well as the craft and techniques used in the making of glass and crystal. In 1769, an Englishman named William Stephens took over the management of the failing Marinha Grande Royal Glass factory, going on to make it one of the most prestigious factories in the land.

CHAPTER SEVEN

TRAVEL, HEALTH, & SAFETY

ENTERING THE COUNTRY

Citizens of countries in the European Union traveling to Portugal require only a valid identity card to enter the country. Visas are not required for citizens of countries included in the Schengen area or those who have signed conventions with Portugal, such as Brazil, Canada, and Colombia.

During the Covid-19 pandemic, all incoming travelers were required to show proof of vaccination or a negative PCR test in order to enter the country; however, all entry restrictions were dropped in July 2022, including for the Azores and Madeira. Travelers are, however, advised to check online before travel for the latest information regarding entry requirements. At the time of publication, face masks remain mandatory in health care facilities.

FLYING

Portugal's national airlines operating domestic,
European, and intercontinental routes are TAP
and Sata, while TAP Express (formerly Portugalia)
operates nationally and within Europe. Most of the
major international airlines fly to and from Portugal
as well. On the continent, the main airports for
domestic and international commercial flights are
located in Faro, Lisbon, and Porto. In Madeira, there
are airports in Funchal and Porto Santo, and the
Azores airports are on Santa Maria, São Miguel (Ponta

The Dom Luís I Bridge crosses the Douro River, connecting Porto and Vila Nova de Gaia.

Delgada), and Terceira (Lajes). Besides these, there are numerous small airports that handle short-haul domestic flights, but the Lisbon and Porto airports account for more than 70 percent of the country's overall air traffic.

TRAINS

Train travel in Portugal is cheap in comparison with other European countries and offers a convenient and comfortable way to see the country. Portugal's national railway company, CP (Comboios de Portugal), offers extensive daily regular and express options for traveling up and down the country. The high-speed Alfa Pendular route between Braga and Faro is considered one of the best intercity connections in Europe and is the fastest way to reach the major northern or southern cities from Lisbon. For a more leisurely trip, there are regional trains that stop at most stations en route, and intercity trains that stop only at the main cities. Trains heading north leave from Lisbon's Santa Apolónia and Oriente stations. In Porto, passengers can disembark at Campanhã or São Bento, or continue on to stations further north. Southbound trains from Lisbon leave from the Barreiro station on the south side of the Tagus and end in the Algarve. There are also broad networks of local commuter trains.

In September 2022, the Portuguese prime minister announced the construction of a Lisbon-Porto high-speed rail line that will allow passengers to travel between the two cities in just one hour and fifteen minutes. The line is planned to eventually extend to Vigo in Spain, creating a high-speed rail connection along the entire Iberian Atlantic coast. Construction of the new line is due to begin in 2024 and is forecast to be completed by the early 2030s.

The Alfa, Regional, and Intercity trains offer

first- and second-class cars. On all trains, children under the age of three travel free, and those between the ages of four and eleven travel for half the adult fare. Seven-, fourteen-, or twenty-one-day tickets are available at reduced rates for unlimited travel throughout the country. Plan your train journeys and purchase tickets easily using CP's own app, which is available for both iOS and Android phones.

International trains run daily from Lisbon and Porto to Paris (Sud Express), Madrid (Lusitânia), and Vigo. Portugal is also on the InterRail circuit, which links over thirty European countries.

BUSES

Coach travel is also a viable option, with a number of private operators running regular, comfortable, and affordable services.

Rede-Expressos links Lisbon to the main cities of Porto and Braga in the north, and Faro in the south. Renex, a Braga-based company, runs a regular Porto–Lisbon–Algarve route, with departures from the Clérigos Tower, one of Porto's most famous monuments. REDM specializes in the north, running a regular Porto to Bragança route, connecting with Coimbra and Lisbon as well. EVA runs regular routes between Lisbon, Alentejo, and the Algarve.

Bridges and Barges

The commuter traffic to and from Lisbon, the country's principal business center, can be staggering, especially for those who need to cross the Tagus. The 25 de Abril bridge (called the Salazar bridge until 1974), which looks very much like San Francisco's Golden Gate suspension bridge, was inaugurated in 1966 and provided a quick and easy way to cross the river until the ever-growing number of cars eventually turned it into a bottleneck for heavy traffic. In 1999, a lower railway level was added as a way to relieve congestion and provide an alternative to car travel. Another great feat of Portuguese civil engineering is the Vasco da Gama bridge. Inaugurated for the World Expo in 1998, at over 10 miles (17.2 km), it is the longest suspension bridge in Europe. Other than these two bridges, several docks along the Lisbon waterfront service a fleet of fast and modern ferries that provide regular river crossings.

DRIVING

Up until the early 1990s, the roads in Portugal were bad enough to make even the most adventurous tourist reconsider driving. Since then, however, thanks to events like the Lisbon and Porto European

Culture Capital tenures, the network of new roads and highways is excellent and well signed, making car travel virtually anywhere quick and easy. That said, it's a good idea to use GPS or a navigation app, since once off highways and main roads, signage can be confusing or even nonexistent. Waze is the most popular navigation app locally.

The Portuguese are reputedly among the most reckless drivers in Europe, and the accident rate is high. Generally rowdy and aggressive behind the wheel, this is the one time that Portuguese people are always in a hurry, so they tend to overuse their horns as well as their hands and voices. The best advice is to stay calm, maintain a sense of humor, and stick to the right lane. Give others the right of way, even if they're not entitled to it, because they will seldom yield. As most cars are manual transmission, specify at rental if you require an automatic car. Rental cars are also primarily gasoline-powered, so if you want an electric car, this should be specified as well.

Thanks to government subsidies and incentives, Portugal has one of the highest electric vehicle market shares in Europe, with electric and hybrid cars making up close to 40 percent of new car sales in 2022. There are currently more than five thousand chargers across 2,240 locations in Portugal, and the government has committed to quadrupling that number by 2025. For those who would like to rent electric but are unsure of how far they'll make it before their battery runs out, hybrid is a solid choice and is usually available for rent. The initial cost is normally slightly higher than for petrol cars, but the saving on gas can be considerable.

For many Portuguese the car is a prized possession, if only to drive the family around on the weekend. This can make getting around by car on Saturday and Sunday afternoons somewhat frustrating, especially along coastal roads and in small towns, since these can fill with cars that circulate at virtually a walking pace as people take their time to enjoy the views and the drive. Young city-dwellers don't give as much importance to owning a car, however, and are happy to make use of the various other travel options that are available, among them ride-hailing apps, public transportation, and bike sharing options. More recently, free-floating electric scooters have been added as an urban travel alternative. See Urban Transportation on page 157 for more.

Pedestrians beware! Though you have the right of way at crosswalks, drivers and now scooter-riders frequently ignore this, so be careful when crossing busy streets. If driving, watch out for jaywalkers—they come in large numbers and tend to cross anywhere, regardless of traffic. It's also important to now keep an eye out for electric scooters when driving in cities.

Parking

The Portuguese have not taken to the concept of carpooling, so most cars carry only the driver. This causes traffic jams and bottlenecks on highways as well as in the urban centers, and makes above-ground parking difficult to find. There are, however, many underground parking garages spread throughout the cities.

The Portuguese are both creative and liberal with their parking, often occupying pedestrian crossings and pavements haphazardly, as well as gently nudging other bumpers in order to fit into a tight spot. As with driving, though, parking violations are also receiving greater attention and penalties. Parking is illegal on curbs marked with a yellow line. In some cases, an illegally parked car will receive only a ticket, but there are also tow trucks that impound vehicles, and a wheel-clamping system is used in the major city centers. If you're lucky enough to find legal street parking, don't be surprised if passersby stop to watch you maneuver, and may well join in to help by signaling which direction to turn the wheel and when to stop.

In order to facilitate meter parking, there are convenient parking apps, such as ePark in Lisbon and Telpark in Porto, which can be used to pay for parking and for topping up your meter.

Parkers

It is common to come across *parkers* in Portugal's city centers. These are homeless people who have taken to the main streets and populated areas to "help" drivers find parking for their cars. These industrious parking assistants can often be seen waving at empty spaces, with the expectation of receiving compensation for their efforts (usually a 50 cent or 1 euro coin). Giving them money is optional, but if you choose not to, there's a chance you'll find your car scratched or missing a mirror or antenna when you return. If you do pay them, bear in mind that illegal parking spaces remain illegal and subject to fines, towing, or tire clamping, and that parking meters must still be paid.

RULES OF THE ROAD

The Portuguese police used to have a notoriously laid-back attitude toward traffic regulations. This is no longer true. Today's laws have, in fact, become quite strict, and are more aggressively enforced.

All passengers must, by law, wear seat belts. Children under the age of twelve must use appropriate car seats.

It is illegal to use a cell phone while driving, except with an earpiece (which is permitted in only one ear), or a hands-free set. It is also illegal to drive barefoot or without a shirt.

In case of a breakdown, the mandatory triangle must be placed on the road behind the car, and a yellow fluorescent vest must be worn. These should be provided in any rental car.

Drunk Driving

The maximum legal limit for drinking and driving is 0.5 grams of alcohol per liter of blood. If this limit is exceeded, the penalties range from serious fines, immediate impoundment of the vehicle, and license suspension, to prison sentences.

When stopped by the police, the driver must submit a passport or other valid picture identification, a valid Portuguese or international driver's license (with photograph), vehicle registration, proof of ownership, and valid insurance papers. Most traffic police officers won't have strong foreign language skills, so if you do get stopped, chattering away in your native language might well get you off the hook, as long as it is for a minor offense.

Traffic regulations and road signs are the same in Portugal as in the rest of Europe. Driving is on the right-hand side. One should therefore stick to the right lane and use the left lane only to overtake or to turn left. The Portuguese seldom obey this rule, but it's a good one to follow in order to avoid trouble. At junctions, vehicles approaching from the right always have priority, unless they encounter a stop or yield sign. At traffic circles, cars already on the circle have priority.

SPEED LIMITS

Built-up city area 31 miles per hour (50 kmph)

Main roads 56 miles per hour (90 kmph)

Highways 75 miles per hour (120 kmph)

Tolls

All highways have tolls, and the amount paid depends on the distance traveled. The shorter highways have a fixed rate, which is paid immediately, while longer distances will require you to collect a ticket at the first tollbooth and pay when exiting. Stop at the booth marked with a green light. Cash and credit or debit cards are accepted. All tollbooths have at least one fast lane identified with a white "V" (for *Via Verde*, which means "Green Pass") inside a green square. These are only for cars with an electronic toll payment system. Don't use these lanes unless your vehicle has the white toll identification box on the windshield. Your car rental company can provide and activate this device for use on toll roads, which will be connected to your credit card for payment.

URBAN TRANSPORTATION

Lisbon has an efficient underground rail system with four lines: Red, Blue, Green, and Yellow. The metro (marked with a white "M" in a red square) is clean, efficient, and inexpensive, and covers most of the city's center and outskirts, also connecting with buses and commuter trains. All stations have automatic ticket machines with easy-to-follow multilingual instructions. Lisbon's metro was extended and refurbished for Expo '98, and station terminals boast impressive tile murals by renowned Portuguese artists. Two additional metro stations are currently being built in order to connect Lisbon's Green and Yellow lines, and are expected to be completed by 2025.

In Porto, the under- and above-ground metro has six lines that connect the city center with the surrounding suburbs. Both Lisbon and Porto metros run between 6:00 a.m. and 1:00 a.m.

In Lisbon, Carris runs an extensive network of buses, streetcars, and cable cars. Bus stops are identified by posts or shelters displaying maps with the routes and timetables. There are several options for tickets and passes, the most popular among tourists being the Lisboacard, which includes one-, two-, or three-day travel passes plus free admission to certain monuments and museums. Those who plan to use public transportation in Lisbon can download the Carris app, which provides routes and timetables, as does the Move-Me app.

In Porto, STCP runs the buses, streetcars, and cable cars. As in Lisbon, stops have posts or shelters that display route maps and timetables, and the Andante card allows use not only of the STCP transportation, but also of the metro and trains running in and around the city.

Taxis in Portugal have always been black with green tops. When the country entered the European Union, many adopted the EU standard beige color, but this was short-lived, and most taxis are currently still black and green. The base fare is always the same, but there are four different tariffs, depending on the time of day or day of the week (nights, weekends, and holidays being most expensive). Extra is charged for phoned-in requests and for luggage exceeding certain dimensions, but portable child beds, strollers, and wheelchairs are transported free of charge. Within the cities and towns, the taxi's meter must be running, but for longer distances the fare is negotiated in advance and the passenger is required to pay the taxi's return trip as well as all tolls.

As mentioned, there are several convenient ride-hailing apps available for use in Portugal's cities, the most popular among them being Uber, Lyft, and Cabify. Electric scooters are also widely used in city centers; Bolt, Jump (Uber), Voi, Lime, and Bird scooters are currently available for hire in Lisbon and Porto.

Simply download the app of the company whose scooter you want to ride, add your card for payment, scan the scooter's QR code, and off you go. Though helmets are not required, they are recommended, and electric scooters are expected to comply with traffic rules,

Electric scooters are available for hire in Lisbon and Porto.

which means among other things staying off sidewalks except for parking and stopping at red lights. Riders are required to be eighteen or over. Cyclists and scooter-riders should beware: bicycle lanes are a fairly recent addition to Portugal's city streets so drivers aren't always on the lookout for two-wheeled road users.

WHERE TO STAY

While Portugal offers a wide range of national and international hotels on the mainland and islands, with prices and services ranging from basic to luxurious, there are a number of more "typical" accommodation solutions that provide a better taste of Portuguese culture and can be found all over the country.

Pousadas are state-owned historical buildings such as castles, monasteries, and convents that have been restored and turned into exclusive hotels. These offer high service standards while maintaining a strong cultural and regional context.

Estalagens are four- or five-star hotels whose architecture and style also reflect the regional character. Unlike the *pousadas*, however, they are privately owned.

For more affordable accommodation, there are pensions (two to four stars), motels (two or three

stars), and numerous youth and family hostels.
Another popular choice for families is the *aparthotel*,
a hotel consisting of self-contained apartment suites
ranging from two to five stars, with living rooms
and kitchenettes. Here visitors can settle in a more
homelike environment. In 2012, Portugal introduced
important reforms to an extremely outdated lease
law which, in addition to attractive tax benefits for
foreigners, brought a veritable boom to a virtually
non-existent rental market. One of the effects of
this was the mushrooming of short-term rental
apartments, a phenomenon that has swept most
major European cities, providing an alternative
option for affordable tourist accommodation. Many
of these can be found on platforms like Airbnb. A
wave of new hotel developments has also taken place
in recent years, bringing innovative new alternatives
for families and young travelers.

For a more rural and family-oriented setting, there
are TER (*turismo no espaço rural*) guesthouses. These
are generally family-owned manor houses or working
farms that provide contact with nature and the locals.
They must be registered at the State Tourist Office
and receive one of three classifications. TH (*turismo
de habitação*) accommodation refers to manor houses
recognized for their architectural value, TR (*turismo
rural*) guesthouses are homes that reflect the rural
environment, and AT (*agroturismo*) means that the

accommodation is part of a farming estate. Every TER guesthouse must have a metal plaque in the main entrance displaying the TER symbol and State Tourist Office logo.

HEALTH

The Portuguese state provides national residents with free health care in public hospitals and health centers, but these are usually overcrowded, have long waiting lists, and the quality is sometimes questionable. Private health care in Portugal is undoubtedly a superior, albeit expensive option for foreigners, so it's best to have medical insurance in place before traveling.

Though many doctors speak English and/ or French, it's a good idea to have a local friend accompany you to help with communication, especially in an emergency. The national emergency phone number is 112, but, again, it's best to ask a local to place the call. For those who plan to stay in Portugal upwards of a few weeks, it's a good idea to register with your embassy or consulate when you arrive and keep the number close at hand, just in case.

SAFETY

The Polícia de Segurança Pública (PSP) upholds
security in Portugal's cities, while the Guarda
Nacional Republicana (GNR) maintains national
safety and runs the highway patrol (Brigada de
Trânsito).

Violent crime isn't a major threat in Portugal,
but theft is not uncommon. To avoid problems,
it's best to keep doors and windows locked (cars,
hotel rooms, home) and don't leave bags or luggage
unattended. When leaving your hotel for the day,
don't leave money and valuable goods in plain
sight. As with anywhere else in Europe, the usual
common-sense precautions apply.

CHAPTER EIGHT

BUSINESS BRIEFING

PORTUGUESE BUSINESS CULTURE

Portugal is a country of contrasts and contradictions, and this is especially true in the professional arena. The business fabric is very diverse, even within the same field, with small, family-run businesses at one end of the spectrum and large multinationals at the other. Tempting as it may be to try to generalize and stereotype the business sphere, if you're working in Portugal, it's important to adapt your approach to the particular company you'll be dealing with.

The average Portuguese employee upholds a "work to live" rather than a "live to work" ethic. The office is where one goes to make a living, while the more important aspects of life take place elsewhere. In business, as in their private lives, the Portuguese are individualistic and tend to concentrate on short-term rewards rather than long-term results. They are generally reluctant to take risks for fear of negative consequences, and avoid taking responsibility, preferring to pass decisions along to those in superior positions.

This apparent lack of accountability or commitment can be exasperating, but if successfully motivated and won over, Portuguese people are hardworking and fiercely loyal. In order to obtain cooperation, it's important to give the business at hand a personal angle; for example, you should ask the person for their help rather than make them feel that they are fulfilling an obligation. When this is achieved, their resourcefulness and flexibility will surface, but only if they feel that they are helping themselves or doing someone a personal favor, rather than handling a professional situation.

Young professionals are beginning to challenge the traditional way of doing business in Portugal, in large part by pushing for more open and participatory workplaces. As a result, the local business culture is slowly becoming more openminded and team-oriented, creating a more flexible and professional environment. While young professionals in Portugal may be more committed to the development of their careers and work environment than their predecessors, they continue to see great value in maintaining a healthy work-life balance.

Desenrascado

Portugal's business landscape is comprised primarily of small and medium-sized companies, or PMEs (*pequenas e médias empresas*), as the Portuguese call them. Many of these have been family-run for generations, with leadership passed on to relatives with little or no formal business training. For this reason, the Portuguese work ethic and habits can strike outsiders as unconventional and quite unprofessional. On the other hand, this unpredictable infrastructure, where job descriptions are often unclear, has made the Portuguese very good at multitasking, and extremely resourceful at problem solving. This flexibility and ability to think and act quickly under pressure, referred to in Portuguese as being "*desenrascado*," is a highly valued characteristic. The more d*esenrascado* you are, the more respect you will command from your colleagues.

Cunhas

Another vital feature in Portuguese business is connections, or "*cunhas*" (pronounced "*coonias*"). A suspicious people by nature, the Portuguese rely heavily on networking and connections to open doors. In many companies, to their own detriment, who you know is still more important than what you know, and the higher up in the organization your acquaintance is, the better. Name-dropping is common practice, and people show how well connected they are, or find out how well connected others are, by doing just that.

The main industries that have resulted from tradition and favorable natural conditions are textiles, footwear, cork, pulp and paper, wine, and tourism. Recently, however, other business areas have evolved, such as the IT, auto, and electronics industries, paving the way for new business trends. The growing influx of multinational organizations has also substantially broadened horizons and raised business standards and practices, as well as bringing a boom in the business services sector.

LABOR

In many ways, some of the Portuguese population's character traits carry over into the country's workforce: undemanding and unambitious, yet loyal and resourceful. Overall, unionization levels are low, even in the traditional heavy industry sectors such as metalwork, chemicals, and shipyards, and contact between the workers and syndicates is minimal. Curiously, the unionization level is unusually high in the banking sector (over 80 percent), due mostly to the special access provided to private medical care. The unions intervene very little in daily management and rarely exercise their right to information in various administrative decisions. Their role is more to oversee collective agreements and ensure these are implemented accordingly.

There are two national syndicates, the CGTP and the UGT, and these differ greatly politically and socially. The CGTP, the more activist union, represents primarily the blue-collar industry and public service sectors. The UGT focuses more on the private business sphere, with wider representation of white-collar workers, such as in the service and tourism sectors. Alternatively, individual companies may choose to develop their own labor policies and programs, using government laws as a starting point.

COMPANY STRUCTURE AND ORGANIZATION

Most Portuguese firms are either corporations, Sociedade Anónima (S.A.), or private limited companies, Limitada (Lda.). Organizations generally have a pyramid infrastructure, with an administrator or board of directors at the top, followed by the general manager, middle managers, and employees at the bottom. This hierarchy is rigid, clearly defined, and strictly followed. People do not step on each other's toes, so one must go through all the appropriate channels and be prepared to wait to get even the simplest tasks accomplished.

A typical workday begins anywhere between 8:30 a.m. and 10:00 a.m., depending on the type of business, and ends between 4:30 p.m. and 7:00 p.m. The Portuguese are not known for their punctuality, however, so although foreigners are expected to be on time, they in turn should be prepared to wait! As discussed in Chapter 5, numerous coffee breaks are taken throughout the day, and lunches can last as long as two hours. When in Portugal for business, stay alert, since negotiations and other matters may suddenly be resumed during these supposed timeouts. Deciding when to end the day can prove tricky. While leaving early or on time is met with disapproval, those who remain the latest are seldom the most productive.

Deadlines are considered a necessary formality not to be taken too seriously or literally and are rarely met. Be sure to set a date that allows some leeway to get the job done when you need it. Even once a delivery date is established, phone ahead to ensure your business has not been forgotten or placed on the back burner.

CONTRACTS AND FULFILLMENT

Care should be taken when drafting and agreeing upon contracts. Portugal's legal system is based on Roman civil law and the Napoleonic Code, in which a complete existing body of law is applied to all cases. Portuguese contracts are therefore shorter and simpler than those drawn up under British common law because certain areas are already covered by the country's civil code. That said, growing foreign business and investment has brought a more Anglo-Saxon influence to some contracts in Portugal, thereby making them more extensive. US and British contracts, based on common law, tend to be longer and more elaborate because of the need to cover every eventuality.

Though this varies from sector to sector and company to company, contracts in Portugal are generally regarded as binding. However, in a country where a gentleman's agreement and a handshake still carry weight, it's not always necessary to revise contracts to cover small details. The Portuguese are not litigious by nature and will give each other the benefit of the doubt if the need for a small alteration arises. As we've seen, however, deadlines are often missed, even when stipulated in a contract, so be sure to set clauses that protect you in case of delays (for example, penalties or termination of the contract).

COMMUNICATION STYLE

Portuguese written communication in business tends to be formal and long-winded, though this has changed with the growth of e-mail. During first meetings, the Portuguese adopt a certain formality and stiffness as much as a sign of respect as to indicate where each stands on the hierarchical ladder. With such a delineated hierarchy, the boss (*patrão*) tends to condescend to employees, and in return is accustomed to a degree of flattery and praise. If managed with subtlety, this is expected and appreciated.

Titles carry great significance in Portugal, and it's important to use them. Anyone with a generic university degree is entitled to use "Doctor," so at work Maria Silva will be referred to as "Doutora Maria Silva." If someone has a more technical degree, then that title is used. A male architect is called "*Senhor Arquitecto*," a female engineer "*Senhora Engenheira*," a male professor "*Senhor Professor*," and so on. Although the entry of a great number of multinational companies to Portugal, as well as the emergence of new companies run by younger Portuguese, have reduced the formality in business environments, it's safer to maintain the more respectful *você* form in professional situations, unless your partner switches to the *tu* form (see Chapter

9 for more). At first meeting, don't call someone by their first name unless they insist or do the same.

Keep it Personal

Begin face-to-face or telephone communication by showing interest in the person's general well-being and personal life. The more details you remember (birthdays, children's ages), the more the person will warm to you. As previously mentioned, the Portuguese have a penchant for talking about their ailments in vivid detail, so inquiring about their health is guaranteed to score points. Also offer personal information about yourself, telling something about your life, family, or country. Take the time to engage in conversation and find common ground with the people with whom you intend to work, thereby creating a personal as well as professional relationship.

PRESENTATIONS AND NEGOTIATIONS

The Portuguese welcome presentations as a break from the regular work routine, but before long will begin worrying about how this is going to extend their workday. Thus, it's important to keep presentations short and to the point. Be confident and self-assured, without being cocky. Make eye

contact and be prepared to negotiate down from
your opening bid. Visual aids can be useful and
create a good impression, but avoid distractions
or anything that may prolong the presentation
unnecessarily.

As a general rule, the decision-making process
in Portuguese companies is highly centralized, and
ultimately the responsibility of the managerial or
administrative levels. With such a clear hierarchical
structure, it's usually easy to determine who the
decision-maker is in a group. Concentrate the
arguments on that person, though not in a way that
disregards the other people present. Once you are
past the presentation phase, be prepared to wait.
The fear of taking responsibility for making the
wrong decision is great, and all other options and
alternatives will be explored before a final decision
is made.

TEAMWORK

Given their strong hierarchical structure and
inherently individualistic nature, teamwork has
not traditionally been a prominent feature in
traditional Portuguese companies. With the influx of
dynamic young professionals and increased foreign
investment, however, workplaces are evolving and

adopting more inclusive and participative work methods that more openly embrace teamwork. In older companies, where the pace of change is slower, the importance of family and social life makes being part of a team come naturally, but be sure to define each team member's responsibilities clearly.

DRESS CODE

The dress code in business depends greatly on the field in question. Whereas in finance or law a formal business style of dress is adopted, in areas like advertising or tech, people are more laid-back. When in doubt, it's safer to err on the side of business formality, with men wearing a suit or blazer and tie, and women avoiding short skirts and low-cut tops. It's best to refrain from wearing jeans and sneakers until you've managed to gauge the company's dress code.

BUSINESS ENTERTAINING

The Portuguese love to socialize and entertain, so make yourself available for meals and drinks. While it's not uncommon to be invited to someone's home to meet the family, most business entertaining takes place in the country's best restaurants. Bear in mind that many deals are closed across the dinner table. A relaxed atmosphere takes the edge off business, and the Portuguese are very good at using this to their advantage. As for the bill, whoever entertains, pays. Thus, a foreigner visiting Portugal is considered a guest, but if a second visit is made, you should reciprocate.

WOMEN IN BUSINESS

Women have made great progress in the business world, especially where equal opportunity is concerned, with a growing number of women assuming top positions in companies and politics. The general consensus, however, is that changes at the top are not mirrored at lower rungs of the ladder and that men still largely have the upper hand, a sentiment that is backed up by a persistent gender wage gap that in 2022 was around 11 percent. Thus women have to make much more of an effort to be heard in the boardroom, and their professional progression is generally slower than that of their male counterparts, although this situation has evolved in certain sectors such as law, services, and finance. Nonetheless, once a woman has children, it is generally agreed that her career will slow down significantly, and Portugal is quite far behind other European countries in this respect. Paid parental leave is a mere five months, day care facilities on company premises are virtually nonexistent, and there are very few incentives to keep a working mother in the workplace. However, while in the past part-time work and working from home was rarely accommodated, workplace changes brought about by the Covid-19 pandemic mean that many are now more able to achieve a work-life balance that allows them to attend to the needs of their young children at home without having to sacrifice their careers.

CHAPTER NINE

COMMUNICATING

THE PORTUGUESE LANGUAGE

Portuguese, spoken by an estimated 260 million people, is the official language in seven countries around the globe. These are Portugal, Brazil, Angola, Mozambique, Guinea-Bissau, Sao Tomé and Príncipe, and Cabo Verde. The language is also still widely spoken in former colonies such as Macau, East Timor, and Goa.

The Portuguese language has its earliest roots in Latin and Galician, with influences from Germanic and Arab dialects. During the Renaissance, its vocabulary and grammatical structure was further enriched by Greek. In the fifteenth century, extensive maritime travel brought contact with French and English, which would also contribute to modern Portuguese.

European Portuguese is a difficult language to learn. It's fast and throaty, and is curiously often confused with Slavic languages such as Russian or Polish. The Portuguese speak quickly, with vowels or even entire syllables "eaten up" or lopped off for the sake of brevity. A colorful range of slang and popular expressions makes the language even more challenging to learn. Still, though accents vary from north to south, the situation is not like that found in Spain, where the number of dialects renders the language incomprehensible from region to region. The main regional differences in Portuguese lie in pronunciation and popular expressions. In the north, the letter "v" is pronounced "b," and vice versa. In Madeira and the Azores, the accent is completely different, but with such a regular flow of tourists visiting all year round, many of the locals speak at least rudimentary English.

Most language schools abroad offer Brazilian Portuguese rather than European Portuguese, probably because the former is easier to speak and understand. Listening to both, it can be hard to believe that Brazilian is actually the same language. It's spoken much more slowly, with every letter and syllable enunciated and sung, rather than the clipped and more Slavic-sounding European Portuguese. The difference between the two could be compared to European French and Quebecois.

Passionate about Brazilian music and TV shows, virtually all Portuguese understand Brazilian and are good at imitating it, whereas many Brazilians have some difficulty understanding the European version of their mother tongue.

GETTING BY

In the more popular tourist destinations, most locals speak English, if only at a basic level, and in the Islands and the Algarve, many have a grasp of French and German as well. French was the second language taught in schools up until the 1990s, but since then English has been given greater emphasis. The influx of North American culture has also increased the younger generations' grasp of English and with the growing number of multinational companies in Portugal, as well as many people choosing to study abroad, this trajectory looks set to continue. Nonetheless, if an effort to speak Portuguese is made, it's most often appreciated, and any laughing or teasing that may result is certainly not meant to cause offense. In fact, it's a good opportunity to build rapport.

All nouns in Portuguese are either masculine or feminine, and adjectives have a male or female application, with the feminine ending in "a" and the

masculine in "o." For example, the feminine noun
flor, meaning "flower," can be described as *bonita*
(pretty), whereas the masculine noun *jardim*
(garden) is *bonito.*

FORMS OF ADDRESS

On first meeting, people in Portugal can seem
distant and aloof, but once a level of trust is
established, people quickly let down their
guard and readily become more friendly. When
addressing someone, there are three degrees of
formality and your relationship with the person
will dictate which form to use.

As in French and Spanish, there are two
forms of the second-person singular "you." *Tu*
(pronounced "too") is informal, used among peers
and people on an intimate standing. The formal
você (pronounced "vossey"), the equivalent of the
French *vous* or Spanish *usted*, is used toward older
people and in most professional relationships. In
the most formal situations, don't call people "*você.*"
Instead, address a male acquaintance as "*senhor,*"
the equivalent of "sir," or "*Senhor*" followed by his
first or last name when these are known (such as
Senhor Luis, or *Senhor Silva*), while women should
be called "*Minha Senhora*" ("madam"), and then

"*Dona*" followed by the first name, once known (e.g. *Dona Maria*). The letters *nh* together are pronounced "ni," so that "*senhor*" or "*senhora*" are pronounced "*senior*" and "*seniora*." Better yet, use their title if they have one (Engineer, Doctor, Architect), followed by their name.

Since the *tu* form and first-name basis are only adopted once there's a certain level of familiarity, it's best to follow your interlocutor's lead and switch to informal styles only when he or she does. If the other person is significantly older, he or she would adopt the *tu* form with younger people, but would expect to be called "*você*" or "*senhor/a*" by them.

When answering the phone, the Portuguese say "*sim*," or "*estou*" (pronounced "shtow" and meaning "I am here"), or "*está lá*" (pronounced "tah lah" and meaning "is anyone there?"). After saying goodbye, they often say, "*com licença*" (excuse me) before hanging up.

FACE TO FACE

The Portuguese are very expressive, and extremely good at face-to-face communication. People gesticulate to add emphasis to their words; hands and bodies are in constant motion, and the eyebrows, nose, and mouth are all involved. With strangers or in unfamiliar situations, people tend to be more discreet, but once they're at ease, conversation and laughter generally become more animated.

The Portuguese are a very touchy-feely people, too. They like to stand close to the person they're talking to, and find it natural to touch the other person as they speak. Greetings and farewells between men usually involve many firm hugs and pats on the back, while women often grasp each other's arms and hands.

Avoiding eye contact is guaranteed to arouse suspicion, so be sure to look your conversation partner in the eye, and give a firm handshake.

In a crowded place, or if someone is trying to squeeze past you, don't be alarmed or annoyed if they grab your waist or arm and physically move you aside, while saying "*com licença*" ("excuse me"). Lines are seldom orderly, with people standing very close to the person in front of them and jostling for position. People were more space-aware at the height of the Covid-19 outbreak, but old habits die hard.

In general, it's a good idea to refrain from using vulgar language, especially around women, even when relationships have evolved to a more familiar level.

TYPICAL GESTURES

As you've by now gathered, the Portuguese enjoy using facial expressions and body language when they talk, and it's quite common for someone to actually stand up and move around when telling a story. All this emphasises how important communication is to Portuguese people—the more animated and vivid the better. Here are some local gestures that you should be aware of:

- "Let's go": tap the back of the left hand with the right hand.
- In cahoots: rub both forefingers alongside each other.
- If you suspect you've been told a tall tale: pull lower eyelid down with your forefinger, exposing the lower part of your eyeball.
- If you are telling a tall tale and want to let someone in on it: wink to that person when your victim isn't looking.
- "Wrap it up": cut-throat signal.
- Appreciative or affirmative: thumbs up.
- To insult a man, use the cuckold sign, raising your forefinger and pinky—but do so at your peril!

HUMOR

The Portuguese love a good laugh and are very
ready to ridicule others and themselves in the name
of fun. For entertainment, there's a preference for
slapstick and situational comedy that portrays
ridiculous and often humiliating situations, rather
than dry or ironic humor. Portuguese literature and
fado lyrics with humorous intent can often be dark
and self-deprecating.

While the Portuguese have a good sense of
humor and react well to teasing without too much
embarrassment, family members, particularly
females, are considered off-limits. *Alentejanos*,
people from the Alentejo, who are stereotyped
as being slower and lazier than the rest of the
population, are often the butt of jokes by those
from other parts of the country.

TV, RADIO, AND PRINT

There are four national television networks, two
public (RTP1 and RTP2) and two private (SIC
and TVI), with the private channels carrying the
most sensationalist programming and thereby
achieving the highest ratings. All of the channels
broadcast international shows and series, generally

in the original languages with subtitles. Satellite and cable television is also widely available, providing more than fifty channels of popular national and international broadcasting such as FOX, MTV, BBC World, CNN, Euronews, Eurosport, and Disney. Many today also subscribe to popular digital streaming services like Netflix, HBO, Amazon, among others.

Radio is a popular option while driving, where morning comedy broadcasts that satirize Portuguese society and politics are a favorite. At home the medium of choice is television, with the most popular programs ranging from *novelas*, reality, and talent shows to soccer broadcasts and the news. Popular channels SIC and TVI compete fiercely for audiences through their reality shows, talent shows, and soap operas.

Aside from the major international papers, which are available almost everywhere, there are many local newspapers and magazines. The principal daily newspapers are the more conservative *Diário Notícias* in Lisbon and its equivalent in Porto, *Jornal de Notícias*, while the more liberal is *Público*. The main weekend papers, the *Semanário Económico* and *Expresso,* are more oriented toward the economy and finance. The two main sports-only newspapers, *Record* and *A Bola*, also command a healthy readership. Popular magazines range from society

and gossip publications to fashion and travel titles. Though the Portuguese cultivate a certain conservative restraint in their manner and lifestyle, this attitude contrasts heavily with the graphic depictions of sex and violence in the media.

There are a number of popular online resources for news and current affairs, including the center-right-leaning *Observador*. Among the most popular sites for English-speakers are *The Portugal News* and *Portugal Resident*.

INTERNET AND SOCIAL MEDIA

The Portuguese love electronic gadgets and are extremely enthusiastic about new technologies. Children are encouraged and taught to use computers and the Internet both at school and at home, and most cafés and restaurants offer free Wi-Fi. Avid Internet users, the Portuguese spent on average seven hours and fifty-six minutes online per day in 2022. Asked why they used the Internet, over 70 percent said their principal reason was to keep in touch with friends and family. It's no surprise then that in 2022 around 83 percent of the population had some kind of social media account, which was nearly a 10 percent increase on the previous year, according to DataReportal. Among users aged 16–64, the most popular social media platforms were Facebook, Instagram, LinkedIn, and Pinterest, followed by TikTok, Snapchat, and Reddit. Users reported spending on average 2.5 hours a day on social media. Around 65 percent said that they used the Internet principally to keep up on news and current affairs. Ever savvy and suspicious, almost 76 percent of Portuguese Internet users expressed concern about distinguishing between what was real online and what was fake.

CELL PHONES AND SIM CARDS

Portuguese telecommunications are first-rate, with state-of-the-art technology and services. Three main providers offer affordable packages that combine Internet, cable television, and mobile service. These are MEO, NOS, and Vodafone.

If you're staying in Portugal long term, you'll eventually need a local phone number to do anything from registering for government services to booking a dentist appointment.

Portugal's country code is 351, and all national phone numbers have nine digits, usually beginning with the number 2 or 9. Tariffs vary according to the company but are pretty equal and affordable.

Visitors from outside the EU who are subject to prohibitive roaming charges and who are planning to be in the country for more than a few days should consider buying a pre-paid SIM card on arrival. Vodaphone SIM cards can be purchased on arrival at Lisbon airport, but options are limited. More packages are available in Lisbon proper, where numerous data-only options can also be found. Just make sure your phone is unlocked before arrival.

4G network is available in all populated areas of mainland Portugal. The rollout of 5G began in 2021 following a lengthy frequency auction process, and as of 2023, is ongoing.

POSTAL SERVICES

The mail service in Portugal is modern and reliable. Portuguese post offices, marked with "CTT" in white letters against a red background, generally operate from 8:30 a.m. to 6:00 p.m. on weekdays, with some open on weekends, but schedules can change depending on the location. Mailboxes can easily be found throughout the cities, with regular mail going in the red boxes and express mail in the blue. Stamps can be purchased at post offices from the

Portuguese mailboxes. Red is for regular delivery and blue for express.

service counter or automatic stamp machines as
well as many newsstands and bookshops. Since one
can do virtually anything at the post office, from
paying utility bills to dealing with parking tickets,
lines can get quite long. With stamps available in so
many other locations and a vast network of ATM
machines and Internet solutions that also permit
various types of payments, it's usually better to
explore other options rather than wait in line at
the local CTT office.

CONCLUSION

As you will probably have gathered by now, the
Portuguese are as contradictory and confounding
as their environment. Older generations who
are unwavering in their traditional values and
principles live in harmony alongside a young
population thirsty for change. While some brood
on what could have been and dwell on *"saudade"*
for the past, others look to the future with hope,
and join in an effort to assert themselves at
home and in the world. Historically a daring and
courageous people, the Portuguese continue to
welcome modernization and self-improvement.

With family at the core of their social life, the
Portuguese can at first appear suspicious and even

unfriendly toward strangers. This book has sought to offer advice on how to blend in and melt their reticence to reveal a nature that's warm and fun-loving.

Join them at the table or participate in their celebrations, and they'll teach you how to relax and find pleasure in the simplest things. Explore their cities, seaside towns, and countryside, and you'll discover a fascinating, multilayered, and rich history. Portuguese people, once they are assured that your intentions are genuine, will take you under their wing and reward you with loyal and lasting friendship.

USEFUL APPS

Travel and Transportation

Hail-a-ride with **Uber**, **Bolt**, or **FreeNow**. Rent a scooter with **Bolt**, **Lime**, **Bird**, or **Jump (Uber)**.

Plan your journey and view public transit timetables on **Moovit**. Navigate with **Waze** or **Google Maps**.

Buy rail tickets with **CP** (Comboios de Portugal).

Pay for parking with **ePark** (Lisbon) and **Telpark** (Porto).

Navigate Lisbon's buses with **Carris**.

Find long-term accomodation rentals with **Imovirtual**. For short-term accomodation, there's **Booking**, **eDreams**, and **Airbnb**.

Food, Shopping, and Entertainment

Have meals delivered with **Bolt Food**, **UberEats**, **Glovo**, and **Comer em Casa**.

Order groceries for delivery with **Auchan** (you can use your passport no. if you have no Portuguese VAT ID no.), **Intermarche**, and if you're in the Algarve, **Apolónia**. For organic produce, **Mercearia Bio** deliver mainland-wide.

Portugal's most popular online marketplace for new and second-hand products is **OLX**, where most things legal can be found. Locals also use **Vinted** for buying and selling pre-loved items.

See what's on with **Time Out Lisbon** and **Time Out Porto**. Plan your itinerary and get ideas with **Lisboa Cool**.

Surfers can check conditions with the **Magic Seaweed Surf Forecast** app.

Communication and Media

Brush up on your Portuguese with **Duolingo** or **Babbel**.

Keep abreast of current events with **The Portugal News**.

Portuguese favor all the usual suspects when it comes to social media: **Facebook**, **Twitter**, **Instagram**, **TikTok,** and **Snapchat.**

FURTHER READING

Carreira, Leandro. *Portugal, The Cookbook*. New York: Phaidon, 2022.

Cave, James. *Moving to Portugal Made Simple*. Edinburgh: Marchmont Publishing, 2021.

Crowley, Roger. *Conquerors: How Portugal Forged the First Global Empire*. New York: Random House, 2015.

Disney, A.R. *A History of Portugal and the Portuguese Empire*. Cambridge: Cambridge University Press, 2009.

Hatton, Barry. *The Portuguese: A Revealing Portrait of an Inconspicuous and Fascinating Country*. Clube do Autor, 2012.

Hatton, Barry. *Queen of the Sea: A History of Lisbon*. London: Hurst, 2018.

Page, Martin. *The First Global Village: How Portugal Changed the World*. Alfragide: Casa das Letras, 2012.

Pessoa, Fernando. *The Book of Disquiet*. London: Penguin Classics, 2022.

Saramago, Jose. *Journey to Portugal*. London: Vintage. 2002.

Taborda, J and Bryson, L. *Lisbon Like a Local: By the People Who Call It Home*. New York: DK Eyewitness, 2022.

Woolf, Simon J., and Opaz, Ryan. *Foot Trodden: Portugal and the Wines that Time Forgot*. Massachusetts: Interlink, 2021.

Zenith, Richard. *Pessoa: A Biography*. New York: Liveright, 2021.

ONLINE RESOURCES

www.moving-on.co
Practical information for foreigners moving to Portugal.

www.visitportugal.com
Official Portuguese tourism Web site.

www.portugalglobal.pt
General information for tourism and trade.

www.getgoldenvisa.com/moving-to-portugal-the-definitive-guide
Information for those considering moving to Portugal.

www.portugal-live.net
Online holiday guide.

www.portugalvisitor.com
Resources, services, and city guides for visitors.

www.portugalvirtual.pt
Detailed information for business and pleasure.

www.portugalinbusiness.pt
Promotes Portuguese trade abroad.

www.farmaciasdeservico.net
Locate 24hr pharmacies.

www.cp.pt
Book tickets and check timetables of Portugal's national rail service.

www.carris.pt
Lisbon public transit.

www.stcp/en/travel
Porto public transit.

PICTURE CREDITS

Cover image: *Yellow vintage tram in Lisbon.* © Shutterstock by Olga Gavrilova.

INDEX

Acknowledgements

The author would like to thank Nick, Thomas, Vasco, and Wendy for their valuable support and suggestions.